ONE HUNDRED YEARS OF POLISH DIPLOMATIC PRESENCE IN THE UNITED STATES: 1919–2019

MARIUSZ M. BRYMORA

ONE HUNDRED YEARS OF POLISH DIPLOMATIC PRESENCE IN THE UNITED STATES: 1919–2019

BOSZ

To my Nearest and Dearest
M.B.

TABLE OF CONTENTS

11
Introduction

13
A Concise History of Poles in America

29
Beginnings of Diplomatic Relations

51
Into the Second Republic

61
The War Turmoil

71
Under the Communist Regime

95
The New Beginning

119
Afterword

123
Appendix

Foreword and Acknowledgments

There are probably very few, if any, countries in the world which could be considered as good allies of Poland as the United States of America. The intense relationships between the two states, developed over a time which abounded in events that substantially changed the world's history, would without a doubt provide enough material for a series of books and a multitude of films. Thus, the present publication does not try to cover the complete history of Polish American diplomatic ties. All it aims at is to present the highlights of the activity of Polish diplomats in the United States whose fate and fortune were influenced so much by the developments in Poland, Europe and the World throughout the 20th century. It is a subjective selection of the author whose aim was to give the Reader a companion to Polish diplomatic service in the United States on the occasion of the centennial of its origin.

I would like to express my sincere gratitude and thanks to the Kosciuszko Foundation in New York whose engagement and support made this publication possible. I am very grateful to Richard Porebski, Anna Fedisz, Małgorzata Cup and Piotr Rogulski, the late Albert Mogzec, Władysław Zachariasiewicz and Wanda Spasowski, the Polish Music Center at USC in Los Angeles, the Hoover Institution at Stanford University, the Embassy of Poland in Washington D.C., *Dziennik Związkowy* in Chicago, the National Digital Archives and the Princes Lubomirski Foundation in Warsaw for providing the images presented in the book. I extend my appreciation to all my Polish and American friends and colleagues whose encouragement was instrumental for me throughout the completion of this project. Last but not least, my special thanks go to Filip and Anna, my kids and personal language advisors, and to Dr. Roman S. Czarny from the University of Kielce for his invaluable assistance and advice.

Warsaw, February 2019

Introduction

It is believed in the United States that one of the oldest stories about Foreign Service is the one about the American Ambassador to London from the beginning of the 20th century. One night he went out for a walk. Wandering up and down without any apparent reason, he attracted the attention and even suspicion of a policeman. "What are you doing here?" the police officer asked him. "Taking a walk," the diplomat answered. "Why don't you go home?" asked the bobby. "I have no home," said the man, "I am the American Ambassador."

It is quite a true reflection about the uniqueness of the job of a diplomat, who for most of the professional career keeps changing places and leads the life of a wanderer.

At the time when the Polish-American diplomatic relations were just sprouting, a journalist from *The New York Times* made an observation which seemed to hit the nail on the head when it comes to every diplomatic mission.

"When an Ambassador arrives at his post," William Du Puy wrote, "he soon finds forty or fifty invitations have come in from representatives of other countries. He must accept them if he is to serve the purpose for which he was sent abroad. If he accepts, he must reciprocate. He must entertain. But if he does so in a way that is other than correct in the given circumstances, he humiliates himself and discredits his country in the eyes of representatives of other nations."[1]

---

1 *The New York Times,* William Du Puy: *Uncles Sam's Homeless Diplomats*, February 10, 1924.

Attractive on the surface and very challenging in real life – such is the job of a diplomat. One could reiterate here numerous sayings pertaining to the specifics of this profession to prove how unique and demanding it is but it is enough to bring up just one: "A diplomat is a person who can tell you to go to hell in such a way that you actually look forward to the trip."

The year 2019 marks the centennial of Polish-American diplomatic ties, an occasion which naturally tempts one to make all kinds of wrap-ups and evaluations. These hundred years abounded in numerous historical events and developments, not only in the lives of the two states but also in the history of the world. How did they influence the presence of Polish diplomats in America? How did Polish ambassadors and consuls manage to go through historic junctures? Did they handle the crises well? The chapters below try to take the Readers through the most important moments of the diplomatic history of Poland in the U.S. with the hope that what they read will encourage them to find out more about the fascinating world of diplomacy.

A Concise History
of Poles in America

Whatever source of information on the Polish diaspora one uses, there is no doubt about one thing-the largest Polish community outside their own country has always been in the United States of America. People fled Poland to America to look for better living conditions, to avoid persecution of the occupying forces or to find freedom when the Communist authorities decided to suppress the "Solidarność" (Solidarity) movement by the imposition of martial law. For Poles, America has always been an icon, a country which served as a model of democracy, tolerance, and equal rights, as well as the subject of their dreams about getting rich and hence the goal of their journeys in quest for freedom and prosperity. A unique proof of these Polish feelings for America and the Americans are the 1926 Polish Declarations of Admiration and Friendship for the United States. It is a richly illustrated collection of 111 manuscript volumes, compiled in Poland and delivered to President Calvin Coolidge on July 4, 1926 to honor the 150th anniversary of the Declaration of Independence. From the highest state officials, through business people, members of the military and the clergy, to students of numerous Polish secondary and elementary schools – altogether over five and a half million people signed the Declarations in which they said:

"We, the People of Poland send to you, citizens of the great American Union, fraternal greetings, together with the assurance of our deepest admiration and esteem for the institutions which have been created by you. In them liberty, equality, and justice have found their highest expression and have become the guiding stars for all modern democracies."[2]

---

2 *Polish Declarations of Admiration and Friendship for the United States*, volume 1, Library of Congress, Washington D.C.

This hymn of praise for America and gratitude for the aid Poland received ends with an exclamation: "Long Live the United States of America! Long Live Liberty, Equality and Justice!" No other nation has ever honored the U.S. with such a gift.

At the beginning of the year 2000, a Polish Consul from Chicago was invited by the University of Nebraska in Kearney to give a talk on political, social, and economic transformations in Poland after 1989. Before leaving Chicago he asked the organizers whether they thought it

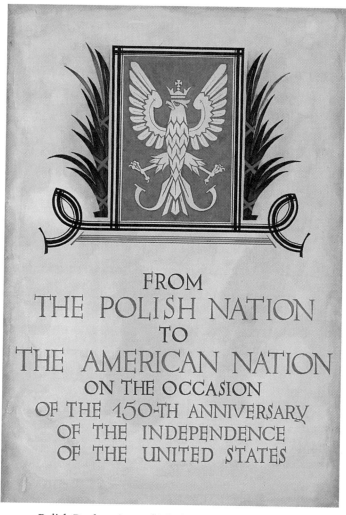

Polish Declarations of Admiration and Friendship
for the United States from 1926. Title page.
Source: Library of Congress.

would be possible for him to meet some local Polish Americans, if there were any at all in that area. The following morning, he received a few similar e-mails. "Polish Americans?" they all said, "there are plenty of them around." The organizers were so efficient that they even found a Polish priest, father Stanley Gorak, to accompany the Consul and be his guide to Polish Nebraska. And so the party set out for a meeting with the local Polish-American community and some 40–50 miles north of the I-80 Interstate they reached a tiny town of Loup City. To his great

Polish Declarations of Admiration and Friendship
for the United States from 1926. Preamble page.
Source: Library of Congress.

amazement, at the edge of the town the Consul spotted a huge wooden obelisk with an inscription: "Welcome to Loup City – Polish Capital of Nebraska; Polish Days June 9, 10, 11". From Loup City they went on to an even smaller village of Ashton where quite a big group of Polish Americans was patiently waiting for the Consul in front of a little wooden house of which they all were very proud. A few months before they had bought the place and founded there the Polish Heritage Center to house a library and a small exhibit which displayed a number of Polish artifacts, including books, photographs, folk decorations and even... Polish tissues. Americans say about places like Loup City or Ashton that they are "in the middle of nowhere". Even though it seems very true about both the locations, the people in Ashton greeted the Consul warmly as if they were the center of Polish life in America. They wanted to show how proud they were of their Polish roots, especially that it was the first chance for them to meet an official representing the country of their great great-grandparents. How did they all get there, then? Nebraska was admitted to the Union shortly after the end of the Civil War, in 1867. At that time the American government, wanting to encourage people to move west, gave away land on the territory which today is the State of Nebraska and at that time was the Wild West. Some entrepreneurial Poles from the big cities of the East Coast or from Chicago decided to try their luck. Others followed soon and settled close by simply to overcome the fear of being alone. This was how the first all-Polish settlements were founded in the Cornhusker State. Two and a half centuries later, meeting the fifth or even sixth generation descendants of those people in the wilderness of Nebraska became irrefutable evidence for the Polish Consul that Poles can be found literary on every corner of America.

Mieczysław Heiman – one of the best known and most trustworthy historians of Poles in America-distinguishes three main periods of immigration from Poland:

- Colonial immigration, 1608–1776
- Political immigration, 1776–1865
- Economic immigration, 1865–1975 (i.e. the year of the publication of his book *Polish Past in America*).

First historian of the American *Polonia* Mieczysław Haiman
at a meeting with Polish American journalists in Chicago in 1930.
Sitting at the table is Vice Consul Tadeusz Buynowski.
Source: the National Digital Archives in Warsaw.

While his division is to a large extent symbolic, there do exist certain characteristics of particular periods of immigration. Simultaneously with the time division, Heiman introduced kind of a "qualitative" division of the Polish immigration breaking it up into political (well-educated people who came to the U.S. in pursuit of higher goals) and economic (impoverished and uneducated Poles who came to America empty-handed).

There exist stories claiming that the first Polish explorers came to America even before Christopher Columbus' time. Legend has it that a Pole took part in the Columbus expedition which discovered America, but there is no historical evidence to prove it. Things look much clearer when it comes to the Jamestown colony in Virginia from the beginning of the 17th century. There were no Poles among the group which founded the first permanent English settlement in 1607. However, a year later, on October 1, 1608, the British ship *Mary and Margaret* brought to Virginia a group of 70 settlers and among them four Polish craftsmen who immediately set up facilities for producing glass, pitch, soap ashes and other commodities which they soon started exporting to England. In 1609, they made their name by saving the life of John Smith, the colony's President, who was captured by the Native Americans. Later ships brought to Virginia more Poles who stood out among the settlers both defending the colony against hostile natives and developing their craft. Ten years later, the Poles of Jamestown showed others how to attain civil rights. They went on strike demanding equal rights with the English. Upon the decision of the Company's authorities in London, "it was now agreed (…) that they shall be enfranchised and made as free as any inhabitant there whatsoever: and because their skill in making pitch and tar and soap ashes shall not die with them, it is agreed that some young men shall be put into them to learn their skill and knowledge therein for the benefit of the country hereafter."[3]

Polish peasants, traders and workers were among those who came to New Holland, which later became the State of New York, during the second half of the 17th century. At about the same time first Poles came to New England. One of them was Olbracht Zaborowski who soon became a very wealthy man and was appointed the first Justice of the Peace in Upper Bergen County in New York State. One of his grandsons, Christian Brevoot Zabriskie became Vice President of the Pacific Coast Borax Company. The well-known tourist attraction, Zabriskie Point in the Death Valley was named after him.

Soon afterwards the Poles moved westwards. Accounts from the first half of the 18th century confirm their presence in Pennsylvania, Ohio, and Kentucky. In 1776 and 1777 respectively, two most famous Poles – Tadeusz Kosciuszko[4] and Kazimierz Pulaski[5] – came to America. The purpose of

---

3 *The records of the Virginia Company*, vol. I, p. 251 in Miecislaus Heiman, *Polish Past in America*, Chicago 1974, p. 15.

4 Tadeusz Kosciuszko (1746–1817) – Polish military engineer and leader who became a national hero in Poland and the United States. In 1776, Kosciuszko moved to America where he took part in the American Revolutionary War as a colonel in the Continental Army. He designed and oversaw the construction of the fortifications at West Point. In 1783, in recognition of his services, the Continental Congress promoted him to Brigadier General. After returning to Poland, he led the 1794 Kosciuszko Uprising as Supreme Commander of the Polish National Armed Forces.

5 Kazimierz Pulaski (1745–1779) – Polish soldier and military commander whose life and achievements best illustrate the motto "For Your Freedom and Ours." He fought

their trips was – in Pulaski's own words spoken to President George Washington – "to serve freedom and to live or die for it." The fame of these two Poles in America is enormous. There exist numerous monuments and likenesses; towns and villages as well as endless streets, schools, parks and other places across the country bear their names. It seems that Pulaski leads the unofficial rivalry for popularity between the two simply because his name is easier for Americans to pronounce. Historical sources report that there were about a hundred Poles fighting in the American War of Independence. Pulaski was promoted to a Brigadier General and became the ranking officer in charge of the newly formed cavalry contingent. His subsequent exceptional accomplishments brought him the title of "the Father of the American Cavalry". He was fatally wounded during the siege of Savannah, GA in 1779. Kosciuszko earned his fame not only for serving as the chief military engineer of the Revolutionary War but also for designing West Point fortifications. What is more, upon his departure from America in 1798, he left behind his famous will in which he authorized his friend Thomas Jefferson to use all his American assets to free and educate black slaves.

Meanwhile, in 1790, the first census was organized in America. Its results, even though partial, justify the claim that there were about 500 Poles in the United States at that time. At the turn of the 18th and 19th centuries, a Polish writer Julian Ursyn Niemcewicz spent almost eight years in the United States. He travelled a lot and then described his American experiences in his memoir titled *Under Their Vine and Fig Tree: Travels Through America in 1797–1799, 1805, with Some Further Account of Life in New Jersey*. Niemcewicz became acquainted with President Washington, paid a long visit to Mount Vernon in 1798, and after returning to Poland, published a book which in fact was the first biography of George Washington.[6]

---

in Poland against the Russian domination and then emigrated to America to help the cause of the Revolutionary War. His merits earned him not only the honorary citizenship of the United States (only few people in history received it) but also the title of the Father of the American Cavalry. He was mortally wounded during a cavalry charge in the battle of Savanah.

6 Julian Niemcewicz, *Krótka wiadomość o życiu i sprawach Generała Waszyngtona (Short Message about the Life and Matters of General Washington)*, published in Polish in Warsaw in 1803.

The first half of the 19th century saw a relatively small influx of Poles into America. They were mainly veterans of the Napoleonic Wars and of the Polish November Uprising of 1830. The circumstances of their departure from Poland, as well as the social status they enjoyed there, made them political defectors. In the spring of 1834, a group of over 200 people from Poland were *en route* to America. While still on board of their vessel, they founded the Polish Committee in America which can be considered the first Polish organization in the United States. Also in 1834, the first Polish book (a textbook of English for Poles) was published in Philadelphia and was meant to be used by the students of the first Polish school in the country run by the author of the book, Martin Rosienkiewicz. The first Polish periodical, titled *Poland – Historical, Literary, Monumental and Picturesque*, appeared in New York in 1842, but it was not until 1863 when the first Polish newspaper *Echo z Polski* (*Echo from Poland*) was launched, also in New York.

Starting from the mid-19th century, immigration from Poland gradually acquired an economic character. The first organized groups of Poles who arrived in the United States to seek a better life came to Texas in 1854. Under the leadership of Leopold Moczygeba, a Franciscan priest, they founded a few settlements in the south of Texas and named them after Polish religious symbols, e.g. Panna Maria (Virgin Mary) and Częstochowa (the name of the religious capital of Poland). To this day people of Polish descent constitute a considerable part of the population of Panna Maria which became known as the first Polish permanent settlement in America. In 2011 Bishop John Yanta, a descendant of those first settlers, established a Foundation whose goal is to build a Polish Heritage Center which will

The building of the Polish Heritage Center in Panna Maria, TX in winter 2019.
Image provided by the Polish Heritage Center Foundation.

preserve the history experienced by his ancestors. This 12-million-dollar project is well advanced and should be completed by the end of 2019.

The eighth U.S. census (1860) reported 7,300 Poles in the United States, living mostly in New York State, Texas and California (one third of their total number was west of the Mississippi River). It is generally agreed that the number of Poles disclosed in all the censuses of the 19th century was heavily understated because immigrants coming to the United States were classified on the basis of their citizenship or the harbor where they had embarked ships to America. Many Poles were registered as citizens of the countries which partitioned Poland or as Germans because this was where they most often started their journeys across the Atlantic. The real number of Poles in America at the beginning of the Civil War is estimated at thirty thousand. Most of them lived in the North and, naturally, when the war broke out, they took the side of the Union. About five thousand Poles actually fought in the war, sometimes against one another, but they remained loyal to their respective sides. Among over one hundred Polish officers were a few colonels and three generals, including Union Brigadier Generals Włodzimierz Krzyżanowski[7] and Joseph Karge[8]. In the Confederate States Army the most famous officer of Polish descent was Kasper Tochman[9] who reached the rank of a colonel.

The rising number of Poles, who brought with them the Roman Catholic heritage, was reflected by the foundation of the first Polish church in

---

7 Włodzimierz Krzyżanowski (1824–1887) – Polish engineer, politician and military leader, during the American Civil War a Brigadier General in the Union Army. After the war, he served as the U.S. Treasury in Georgia, Alabama, Florida, Louisiana, The Washington Territory and New York City. His remains were transferred to Arlington National Cemetery on the fiftieth anniversary of his death in 1937.

8 Joseph Karge (1823–1892) – Polish military officer; after being sentenced to death for his participation in unsuccessful revolutions in Poland in 1848, he fled to America. His numerous military successes in the Civil War earned him a promotion to Brigadier General in 1965. Following the war, Karge accepted a position as Chair of the Department of Languages and Literature at Princeton College (later Princeton University) which he held until his death.

9 Kasper Tochman [sometimes spelt Tachman] (1797–1880) American soldier of Polish descent; he served as an officer during November Uprising in Poland. After the defeat of the Uprising, he fled Poland to France and then to America. After the outbreak of the American Civil War, Tochman, a pro-slave farm owner organized the 14th and 15th Louisiana Regiments as part of the famous Louisiana Tigers Brigade. The Polish Brigade fought at Gettysburg. After the defeat of the Confederacy Tochman was nominated Virginia Immigration Commissary.

America – St. Stanislaw Kostka Church in Chicago in 1866. It was soon followed by the Holy Trinity Church (1873) which until today remains one of the most important centers of both religious and social life of Poles in the Windy City.

A huge wave of economic immigration from Poland started in the 1870s. Until the outbreak of World War I, over two million Poles came to America, a vast majority of them through the most famous gate to the Promised Land – Ellis Island. This was also the time when the first Polish organizations in America were founded, including the Polish Roman Catholic Union of America (1873) and the Polish National Alliance (1880), which have been continuously in operation until the present time.

The official census data for the year 1900 reported some 700,000 Poles in America, with Illinois, New York and Pennsylvania being the most Polish states. Only between 1899 and 1915, the time of the highest economic immigration from Poland, over 1.4 million Poles were admitted to the United States. Most of them were young people who came to America to seek a better life. Three partitions of Poland, a number of unsuccessful attempts to regain independence, persecutions by the invaders, and finally poverty along with lack of prospects for a better tomorrow were the main causes responsible for making the 19th century the time of "great emigration" from Poland. The American census of 1910 reported almost 1.7 million Poles, divided into those born in Poland (c. 938,000) and those born in the U.S. whose at least one parent was born in Poland (c. 726,000). These figures, however, were rather conservative and definitely underestimated the actual number of Poles. The Polish National Alliance Calendar for that same year assessed the number of Poles to be over 3 million and listed Pennsylvania, New York, Illinois, Wisconsin and Michigan as the states with the biggest population of Polish Americans. The year 1910 saw the first demonstration of the political power of the Polish diaspora in the United States. From May 10 until May 14, the Polish National Congress was held in Washington D.C. Over 400 delegates, accompanied by a few thousand supporters, manifested their strength in the American capital while their homeland still remained unmarked on the map of Europe. The underlying reason behind the Congress was to unveil the monuments of Kazimierz Pulaski and Tadeusz Kosciuszko, Polish heroes of the American War of Independence.

During World War I, immigration to the United States from Europe, including Poland, significantly decreased, not only because of the turmoil of the Great War that swept across Europe. In 1917, overruling the veto of President Wilson, the Congress passed the so-called Literacy Law. Soon afterwards American ports of entry were equipped with the signs which read: "If you cannot read, do not enter." Surely, the sign proved very effective. Almost a third of Poles who came to America between 1898 and 1914 fell into the category of the illiterate. Nor were they financially fit. On the average, each of them had a dozen or so dollars in their pockets.

At the same time, Polish Americans started acquiring political power. In 1918, Mr. John Kleczka became the first Congressman of Polish descent. Interestingly enough, he represented the GOP while, throughout history, over 75% of Polish representatives in the Congress were Democratic.

By 1920, the population of Poles in America reached 4 million, with major centers in Chicago, Detroit, Milwaukee, Buffalo, Pittsburg, New York, and Philadelphia. At the time when first Polish diplomatic missions were established, *The New York Times* reported that "there are about 4,000,000 [Poles] in the United States, 400,000 living in New York State, and 130,000 in this city."[10] In the 1920s, a considerable number of them returned to independent Poland. At the same time, the American Congress passed the Restriction Acts of 1921 and 1924 which limited the flow of immigrants into the USA. Notwithstanding these facts, the number of Poles in America continued to grow until World War II.

Almost immediately after Poland's regaining independence, some leaders of the Polish community in America realized the crying need to maintain ties with their homeland by supporting education of the young generation of Poles. Szczepan Mierzwa (called Stephen Mizwa in America), a graduate of Harvard and now an associate professor of Economics at Drake University, started his campaign to create "an Endowment Fund to make it possible for future generations in reborn Poland to study in America and learn something about the nation for whose freedom Kosciuszko fought." In 1925, The Kosciuszko Foundation was incorporated in New York with the main goal to raise funds to grant financial aid to Polish students to study in America and American students to study in Poland, to encourage the exchange of professors and scholars between

---

10 *The New York Times, Polish Minister Coming,* 30 August 1919.

Poland and the United States, and to foster closer intellectual and cultural ties between the two countries.

The beginnings were by no means easy. Interestingly enough, it was the Consulate General in New York which offered a helpful hand to Stephen Mizwa. The mastermind of the Foundation describes the outset of his cooperation with the Polish mission on the pages of his book *The Story of the Kosciuszko Foundation. How It Came About*, with the following recollection:

"As we had no money to pay rent, we had to find desk space free of charge. I went to Dr. Sylwester Gruszka, the then Polish Consul General in New York, and told him the story of the forthcoming Kosciuszko Foundation and asked him if he could find desk space for me in the Consulate building, which was then located at 953 Third Avenue, an unglamorous address at the corner of 57th Street.

He said, "Of course! Not only desk space, but the whole front room on the second floor. It faces the Third Avenue El, is very noisy, and we cannot use it. We can lend you a broom, you can sweep it as it has accumulated plenty of dust, and you can move right in!"

"Thank you very much, Mr. Consul General, but we have no desk and no money with which to buy one. Can you find some old desk you can loan us?"

"Yes, of course," was his reply. "In the basement we have several roll-top desks that we discarded. I will ask the janitor to pick one up for you."

"Thank you very much, Mr. Consul General," I said, "but we have no typewriter. Can you find one you can loan us?"

"Of course, no problem," was his reply. "In the basement we have several discarded typewriters and I will ask the janitor to bring one up to your office. You can move in tomorrow and you will be in business."

And so, I moved in the next day to the second floor noisy office at 953 Third Avenue."[11]

The eight years between 1935 and 1943 saw the establishment of important Polish cultural institutions in the U.S. In 1935, the Polish Museum of America was opened in Chicago with Mieczysław Heiman as its first curator. In 1941, Oskar Halecki founded PIASA – Polish Institute of

---

11   Stephen Mizwa, *The Story of the Kosciuszko Foundation. How It Came About*, New York 1972, pp. 61–62.

The founder of the Kosciuszko Foundation Stephen Mizwa
in the first office of the Foundation which was located in the building
of the Consulate General of Poland in New York.
Source: Archives of the Kosciuszko Foundation.

Arts and Sciences of America, and two years later the Pilsudski Institute
started operating in New York. In 1944, over 2,500 delegates came to
Buffalo for the first congress of the American *Polonia*[12]. They established
the Polish American Congress as an organization whose aim was to unite
Polonia and act on behalf of all Poles in America. PAC officially recognized
the Polish Government in Exile, protested against the Soviet Union
annexing the eastern part of Poland, and criticized the Yalta Conference
decisions. Unfortunately, the newly born organization was not able to
influence the position of President Roosevelt and the American
administration in these matters. Its first chairman Karol Rozmarek
promised to back President Roosevelt in his 1944 reelection bid, counting
in return on his support in Poland's fight to retain its pre-war territory.
Unfortunately, the leader of PAC was not aware that the decisions about
new Polish boundaries had already been taken and soon afterwards he

---

12 Polish word used to describe all Poles living abroad.

realized that all he was left with were the promises from the Presidential campaign.

A new wave of Polish immigrants reached America in the years following the end of World War II. Within just a few years about half a million Poles came to the States as political exiles. The end of the war found them either in POW camps on the German territory or somewhere in Western Europe where they concluded their wartime wanderings. They either did not want to go back to their homeland which found itself under the Soviet domination or they actually had nowhere to go back to as their home towns and villages were now part of the Soviet Union. This post-war wave of immigrants introduced the division into the "old" and the "new" *Polonia*. The latter strongly supported the Polish government in London and was openly hostile towards the Communist authorities in Warsaw, whereas some of the old *Polonia* (i.e. those who were born in America of Polish parents) were more likely to accept the new Polish authorities. Luckily, the latter attitude never won among Polish Americans. Even though the new authorities in Warsaw tried hard to convince people to return, Poles in America remained uncompromising and strongly opposed the "new Polish deal." In 1948, the American Congress passed the Displaced Persons Act on the grounds of which over 150 thousand Poles entered the United States.

The 1950s, 1960s and 1970s was the time when immigration of Poles was effectively limited by the communist authorities to cases of family reunification. The birth of Solidarity – the first independent Trade Union Organization in Central and Eastern Europe – and its subsequent suppression following the imposition of martial law in 1981 – brought about the latest wave of Polish immigration to America which is referred to as the Solidarity immigration. Those who came to the U.S. in the 1980s were both intellectuals and workers who, as Solidarity activists, had to flee Poland to avoid persecution by the Communist regime.

The fall of the iron curtain in 1989 and the rebirth of democracy in Poland which followed did not stop the immigration of Poles to America. Between 1991 and 2003, over 200,000 people from Poland came to the United States. The census of the year 2000 reported 9.3 million people of Polish descent (the latest Census of 2010 did not contain the ethnic background question). At present, the biggest Polish communities are located in the states of New York, Illinois and Michigan. Even if Chicago and New York remain the favorite cities for Poles who wish to settle down in America, in the last 25 years a considerable increase of the Polish population was reported in the south-western states (mainly Texas and Arizona) as well as in Florida. The present-day Polish community in the USA is well educated (one third of them hold a Bachelor's degree or higher), quite well off (the average annual income of a Polish family exceeds considerably the national average), and its members enjoy the status of home owners much more often than other Americans.

For many years, LOT Polish Airlines representatives operating in the United States used to say that their planes brought more Poles to America than they took back. However, recent years indicate that we might be witnessing a historical change. Poland has gone through sweeping political, social and economic transformations which thoroughly changed the life of its citizens. It has joined the European Union, becoming one of the biggest member states. The membership in the EU opened for the Polish people the gates to 27[13] other European countries where they can freely settle down and work. On top of that, the Polish currency got so strong against the American dollar that coming to America has lost much of its original appeal. Hence, all traditional reasons for emigrating from Poland to America, i.e. seeking political freedom, economic well-being or escape from regime persecutions are gone. It may well mean that we are just going through a historical turning point which will commence a gradual fall in the number of Poles in America. Even if this proves true, the Polish nation will always retain a distinctive place in the history of the United States.

Apart from the names mentioned in preceding or following paragraphs, the long list of outstanding Polish Americans would have to include: America's greatest bridge builder – Ralph Modjeski, Postmaster General who introduced zip codes – John Gronouski, virtuoso pianist who invented windshield wipers and paperclips – Jozef Hofmann, presidential candidate – Edmund Maskie, designer and sculptor of the Crazy Horse Memorial – Korczak Ziolkowski or the vamp of the silent cinema – Pola Negri.

---

13 When this is written the Brexit negotiations are still going on and leaving the EU by Great Britain is not certain.

It has always been quite a surprise for most Americans when they were told that Mike Krzyżewski, more commonly known as Coach K – the most successful U.S. basketball coach, Steve Wozniak – co-founder of Apple computers, Warren Winiarski, the man who put California on world's wine map by winning the Paris competition with Stag's Leap 1973 Cabernet Sauvignon or actress and wild life activist Stefanie Powers – just to name a few of our contemporaries – are only examples of thousands of Polish Americans who contributed significantly to make America what it is today.

"Kosciuszko and Pulaski contributed ideals and inspirations to the creation of America and Polish immigration has given its brains and labor to America's development" – these words of the first Envoy of the reborn Poland, Prince Kazimierz Lubomirski, were equally true when he spoke them in 1919 as they are today.

Beginnings
of Diplomatic Relations

On October 7, 1918, the Regency Council of the Kingdom of Poland declared independence of the country. On the following day, Józef Piłsudski, the leader od the Polish Legions which he had created in 1914, was released from the Magdeburg prison where he had been detained for over a year for forbiding Polish soldiers to swear a loyalty oath to the Central Powers. Without delay he headed toward Warsaw in a private train. Just three days later, the Regency Council appointed him Commander in Chief of the Polish forces and entrusted him with a mission of creatinga national government. Consequently, on November 16, the Council followed with a decree changing the Department of State into the Ministry of Foreign Affairs, the act which can be seen as the formal beginning of the Polish Foreign Service. In the meantime, on November 11, 1918, Germany signed an armistice agreement with the Allies and World War I ended. As a result of the provisions of the Versailles Treaty Poland returned to the map of Europe after 123 years of partitions. The patriotic struggle of a few generations of Poles, continued against all odds for a century and a half, finally brought about the resurrection of their homeland. Before the United States could actually recognize the newly born Polish State, as the first country in the world, the American government was to play an instrumental role in the process of Poland's regaining her independence.

The untiring and ceaseless efforts of Ignacy Jan Paderewski[14] carried out since his arrival in New York on April 15, 1915, made the American

---

14 Ignacy Jan Paderewski (1860–1941) – Polish composer, pianist, philanthropist, politician and statesman; Prime Minister and Minister of Foreign Affairs of Poland in 1919. He was acclaimed as a musical genius and one of the most charismatic artists of his time. His political and diplomatic activity contributed significantly to the rebirth of Polish independent state in 1918. A year later, on behalf of Poland, Paderewski signed the Versailles Treaty ending World War I. He was one of the greatest men in the history of Poland whom President F.D. Roosevelt called a "modern immortal."

administration get involved in the Polish cause. He made his goal very clear just a week after coming to America, when he addressed the Polish diaspora in New York saying, "I am a Pole, a faithful son of my Homeland. The idea of great and strong, free and independent Poland has always been the content of my existence. Implementing it has always been the only goal of my life."[15]

Indeed his activity in the next couple of years was almost entirely devoted to helping the Polish cause and his efforts proved extremely successful. His close cooperation with Colonel Edward Mandell House let Paderewski convince the American President to support Polish aspirations to reestablish an independent state. In his speech made at the Kosciuszko Foundation dinner celebrating the 10th anniversary of regaining independence, the pianist revealed what was behind President Wilson's first crucial speech delivered to the Senate on January 23, 1917:

> "Not long before the date of the delivery of that message I wrote a memorandum on Poland at the request of Colonel E.M. House. When Colonel House asked me to write the memorandum, I was surprised. I told him I had to give a recital and that I would have to work on my program. However, I worked for four hours on my recital program, then devoted thirty six hours of uninterrupted work to the memorandum on Poland."[16]

When actually addressing the U.S. Senate, Woodrow Wilson stressed, "I take it for granted (…) that statesmen everywhere are agreed that there should be a united, independent, and autonomous Poland."

Colonel House, who by the way was not a military man at all and was given the nickname "colonel" in recognition of his position in the White House, had a huge influence on President Wilson and his foreign policy and it was he who wrote the famous 14-point address for the President. On January 8, 1918, Woodrow Wilson made Poland part of his plan for the world by declaring in point 13 that "an independent Polish state should be erected which should include the territories inhabited by indisputably Polish populations, which should be assured a free and secure access to the sea, and

---

15 Ignacy Jan Paderewski in his speech to *Polonia* in New York, May 22, 1915.
16 *The New York Times*, *Paderewski Tells of Reborn Poland*, May 17, 1928.

whose political and economic independence and territorial integrity should be guaranteed by international covenant."[17] Even though Paderewski's efforts to make it sound even stronger by changing "should" into "must" failed, a powerful signal was delivered to the world from the Capitol Hill. The message was even more meaningful because it was supported by both the Democratic President and the Republican Congress (the GOP won the majority in both chambers in the 1917 election). These events and the official engagement of the U.S. in the cause of Poland's regaining independence earned Paderewski the title of the first Polish diplomat in America. His mission consolidated the bilateral ties between the two countries and prepared the proper grounds for establishing the official diplomatic relations. When in January 1919 Paderewski formed his new government, he immediately notified President Woodrow Wilson and the Secretary of State Robert Lansing about his new position. His letter was answered with a congratulatory cable dated January 22, 1919, in which Lansing was saying:

"The President of the United States directs me to extend to you as Prime Minister and Secretary for Foreign Affairs of the Provisional Polish Government his sincere wishes for your success in the high office which

Testimonial dinner to Ignacy Jan Paderewski under the auspices of the Kosciuszko Foundation at the Hotel Commodore in New York City on May 16, 1928. Source: Archives of the Kosciuszko Foundation.

17 Woodrow Wilson, *Fourteen Points Speech*, delivered to the joint session of the Congress on January 8, 1918.

you have assumed and his earnest hope that the Government of which you are a part will bring prosperity to the Republic of Poland."[18]

The quoted cable became generally accepted as the official and formal recognition of the Polish government in Warsaw by Washington, establishing at the same time diplomatic relations between Poland and the United States. As early as April 1919, the Americans appointed their first Envoy at the Polish capital, nominating for this post a career diplomat – Mr. Hugh Gibson who arrived in Warsaw on April 28. Just a few days later, on May 2, he presented his credentials to the Head of State – Józef Piłsudski.

The first regulations of the Polish Ministry of Foreign Affairs provided for six categories of Polish diplomatic missions. The first set of them in America consisted of the Legation in Washington, consulates general located in Chicago and New York, 2nd category consulates in Buffalo, Detroit and Pittsburgh and a vice consulate in St. Louis. Two of those, in Buffalo and St. Louis, were closed within the next few years. The rest of them stayed in place to go through a long and bumpy road over the next century.

It turned out to be quite a challenge for the newly born Polish state to find appropriate candidates for its diplomats in the United States. While the search for the envoy in Washington was still going on, the government appointed the first Consul General in New York – Konstanty Buszczyński who became the first Polish diplomat in the U.S., not counting Paderewski of course, who despite not being an ambassador can safely be considered the most successful Polish diplomat ever. The consul arrived in New York on board of the *Fabre Line* steamship Canada on June 2, 1919. The Economic and Social Union of Polish Workingmen and Farmers in America organized a reception at the Hotel Pennsylvania on June 22, 1919 to welcome the first official diplomatic representative of Poland in America. Governor Smith and Mayor Hylan of New York sent letters of greetings and congratulations to Consul Buszczyński. The Governor wrote, "I congratulate his [i.e. the Consul's – M.B.] great country on her new found liberty. With her

---

18 *Foreign Relations* 1919, p. 741. Source: Diplopedia Służby Zagranicznej, MFA of Poland.

Paderewski as the Premier of Poland arrives at the
Peace Conference in Paris in 1919; from left to right: Sylwin Strakacz
(Paderewski's Secretary and future Consul General in New York),
Ignacy Paderewski, Jan Ciechanowski (Paderewski's Secretary
and future Ambassador of Poland to the USA), and Major Iwanowski.
Source: the Paso Robles Paderewski Collection, Polish Music Center, USC.

independence won, I am sure a happy and prosperous future awaits her."[19]
The official inauguration of the Consulate took place on August 14 with
representatives of the United States, Great Britain, France, Japan, Sweden,
Norway and many other countries present during the ceremony at the offices
at 40 West Fortieth Street and at a dinner given later that day by Consul
Buszczyński at the Gotham Hotel. Unfortunately, the first Polish consular
officer in America almost immediately fell into the trap of trying to reunite
conflicted Polish organizations and because his efforts turned out to be a
failure, he left for Poland in less than a year after his arrival in New York.

19 *The New York Times*, June 23, 1919.

Paderewski eventually decided to send to Washington Prince Kazimierz Lubomirski who was neither an experienced diplomat nor an expert on America. He was, however, a well-educated member of an influential Polish aristocratic family, who gained political experience while serving 12 years in the legislative body of Galicia, the Austrian part of the then Poland. Right after this nomination was made public on June 1, 1919, *The Washington Post* introduced the Polish Envoy to the American public, writing:

"Prince Casimir Lubomiraki [the name was misspelt in *The Washington Post* – M.B.], who has just been appointed to represent the newly created Republic of Poland in Washington, D.C., is entitled to the predicate of "serene highness," is married, has a family of young children, all under the age of sixteen, by his wife, a countess of the house of Granow-Bodzicka [the correct spelling of the name was Wodzicka from Granow – M.B.], is about 56, and formerly represented certain districts and agricultural interests in the parliament at Vienna. Like the princess, he was born as a great noble of Austria's Polish province of Galicia, and was a distinguished figure in the political life of the dual monarchy until its downfall."[20]

Prince Lubomirski became the first Polish Envoy Extraordinary and Minister Plenipotentiary in Washington. He took a considerable amount of time to get ready for the journey across the Atlantic, eventually arriving in New York on October 29, 1919. He was accompanied by his family and staff, among them Francis Pulaski, grandson of Kazimierz, who was to act as the First Counselor and serve as a reminder of the Polish contribution to American struggle for independence. The *New York Times* welcomed the Polish Envoy with a nice headline: "Prince Lubomiraski [it seems like the Americans always had problem with Polish names – M.B.] Polish Envoy, Here, First Minister to Washington from New Republic Arrives with Wife and Children; Wants Aid from America; Says Whole Nation is Praying for Speedy Recovery of President Wilson." In this big introductory article, the journalist did not fail to notice that "the new Minister had thirty seven cases of champagne among his baggage, which comes into the country free of entry."[21]

---

20 *The Washington Post*, June 1, 1919.
21 *The New York Times*, October 29, 1919.

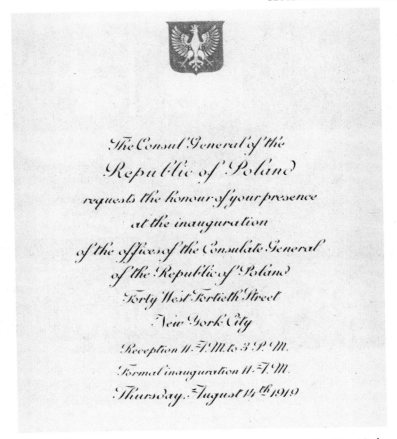

The Consul General of the
Republic of Poland
requests the honour of your presence
at the inauguration
of the offices of the Consulate General
of the Republic of Poland
Forty West Fortieth Street
New York City
Reception 11 A.M. to 3 P.M.
Formal inauguration 11 A.M.
Thursday August 14th 1919

The invite to the inauguration of the Consulate General in New York
– the first Polish mission in the U.S. – on August 14, 1919.
Source: Polish Embassy in Washington Archives,
the Hoover Institution, Stanford University

The following afternoon, the whole party arrived in Washington and on November 1, Prince Lubomirski and other members of the Legation paid a visit to the Department of State. Due to the illness of President Wilson and absence of Secretary Lansing, the Polish Envoy was received by Assistant Secretary of State William Philips to whom he presented a copy of his credentials. Even though Mr. Philips assured his Polish guests that the President was recovering well, it turned out to be impossible to arrange an official presentation of Lubomirski's credentials until the following May when he was finally received at the White House. Only then he got a chance to personally thank the President on behalf of the Polish nation.

Images from the Lubomirski family album showing Envoy Kazimierz Lubomirski with his family during their voyage to America and the interior of the Embassy building soon after it was bought. Source: Private collection of the Princes Lubomirski Foundation.

"It is with the deepest, lasting affection, indeed," he said, "that the people of Poland look to you, Mr. President, who was the first statesman publically to proclaim and espouse the right of my country to be united, to be independent and to have access to the sea, in those state papers whose solemn phrases will be uttered by the lips of generations to come with gratitude and with reverence."[22]

The Envoy's initial task was to find a proper place for the offices of the Polish Legation in Washington. In his report from the beginning of

---

22 Remarks of Prince Kazimierz Lubomirski at the presentation of his credentials to the President of the United States. Source: Polish Embassy in Washington Archives, the Hoover Institution, Stanford University.

December 1919, explaining to the MFA why he decided to buy a property without waiting for a formal consensus, Lubomirski wrote:

"In Washington we experienced real problems in identifying premises that met the Legation's needs, by accommodating both the offices and the Envoy's official residence. We could not fail to observe established local customs in the diplomatic community, which would also satisfy the high expectations towards the diplomatic world of Washington society, to which, one has to say, snobbery was far from an alien consideration. The legation decided to purchase this house without engaging in time-consuming correspondence with its superiors back in Poland, as it constituted a bargain which might easily slip from our grasp."[23]

First Polish Envoy Prince Kazimierz Lubomirski meeting William Hale Thompson, the Mayor of Chicago at the City Hall in Chicago in 1920. Source: Private Collection of the Princes Lubomirski Foundation.

23 Report No 3 of the Polish Legation to the Ministry of Foreign Affairs, December 8, 1919 (the excerpt translated by M. Brymora). Source: Polish Embassy in Washington Archives, the Hoover Institution, Stanford University.

The building he chose, located at 2640 16th Street, has been the seat of the Embassy of Poland since those early days until the present time. The deed between Mary and John Henderson and Prince Kazimierz Lubomirski was recorded on December 23, 1919 and the final cost of the transaction amounted to c. 200,000 USD. Exactly three months later, on March 23, 1920 the husband and wife, Kazimierz and Theresa Lubomirski sold the place to the Republic of Poland for a symbolic sum of ten dollars. Some believe that it was Lubomirski who paid for the mansion out of his own pocket and that he was the donor of the Embassy building to Poland. The more down-to-earth and realistic version claims that at the time of the purchase 40,000 dollars was paid by the Polish government in cash (the money was transferred to the Embassy by the Consulate of Poland in New York) and the rest of the sum became a mortgage on the property. Half of it was paid back in 1932 and the remaining sum two years later. Reacting to press dispatch on the question of the finances, Mr. Sokołowski, the Embassy's Counselor published a statement on December 5, 1934 in which he said that "Prince Casimir Lubomirski, was instructed to act in this matter as the government's representative, and in this capacity signed all the papers in connection with the sale. (…) Prince Lubomirski did not in any way act in his private capacity and many statements to the contrary are erroneous and without foundation in fact."[24]

The building Lubomirski bought is located on the eastern edge of the area of Washington known as Adams Morgan. The recent history of this district of the city is connected with immigration. The vibrant Latino and African communities give an international flavor to this eclectic neighborhood. At the beginning of the 20th century, Mary Henderson, the wife of the Senator from Missouri, was trying to realize her dream of developing this part of 16th Street into the embassy-lined Avenue of the Presidents. Later, however, the district fell in decline. Anecdote has it that there was a time when many taxi drivers, when asked to take someone to the Embassy's address, would look at the passenger rather suspiciously and say, "Are you sure you want to go there?" Today Adams Morgan has acquired its former glamour again and is, in the opinion of many, the best neighborhood in D.C. to live in and dine out.

---

24 *The New York Times,* December 7, 1934.

The Embassy building (undated, most probably from the 1950s or 1960s). Source: the National Digital Archives in Warsaw.

Contemporary view of the Embassy. Photo by Mariusz Brymora.

The story of the Embassy building starts at the beginning of the 20th century or, to be more precise, on April 1, 1909 when the city authorities issued a permit, allowing Senator John Henderson to build a four-story dwelling on the plot of land enrolled in the city record under the number 834, situated on the corner of 16th Street and Fuller. A renowned Washington architect George Oakley Totten[25] designed the building and Fuller Company built it in less than a year. At the beginning of 1910, the structure was completed. In 1911, a magazine titled *The American Architect* published an article about Henderson's place, which not only gave a detailed description of the mansion but also contained some photographs. Thanks to these images we know that the interior of the building is almost exactly the same today as it looked at the beginning of the previous century. The early story of the building is somewhat unclear. Nevertheless, one thing is certain. As early as 1912, and in spite of the fact that they had never lived in it, the Hendersons came to the conclusion that the building was too small. The

25 George O. Totten Jr., (1866–1939) – a native of New York, graduated from Columbia University's architecture program in 1891. He completed his architectural education in Paris and worked in Washington D.C., Philadelphia and other places of the Eastern coast. Apart from the Polish Embassy, he designed in Washington D.C. the University Club (1914), the French and Spanish Embassies, the Congressional Club and many others. He moved to Washington in 1895 and became chief designer at the office of the supervising architect in the Licensure Department. Over the course of his career, he concentrated on designing expensive residences.

modification was again designed and supervised by George Totten. A two-story part, which included the Grand Ballroom, was added and the west-side terraces were turned into additional rooms.

Little is known about the occupants of the building in those early days. In spite of the fact that it was referred to as "the Henderson Embassy building" there is no record of it being used as the seat of a foreign mission. The only mention of its inhabitants can be found in Lubomirski's report quoted above in which he wrote that at the time he was negotiating the purchase of the building the ambassador of Tsarist Russia, Bachmetiew, was residing in it. Even though it seems unlikely that the building remained unoccupied all these years, the street number listings in the directories did not include it until 1920 when the Polish Legation was shown as the occupant.

This white limestone structure is said to represent mainly the French 17th and 18th century architecture with some major additions from the English style (e.g. double-hung windows and the dormer level). Another special aspect of its design are the well-integrated six balconies and two porches. The interior of the house represents mainly English Renaissance, being too florid for styles associated with the continent. As there are quite many additions from other styles as well as some inconsistencies, it might be best to agree that whichever European style in was built in, this style was a little Americanized or "Tottenized" to be precise. Critics claim that almost every room has an architectural problem related to Totten's carelessness. In spite of that, the building remains one of the architect's most coherent works.

Before the visitors enter the Embassy their attention is drawn by the life-sized statue of Ignacy Jan Paderewski standing on the lawn to the left of the main entrance. It was created by a renowned sculptor Jesse Corsaut at the Montgomery Sculpture Center and donated to the Embassy by Harry E. Blythe III – the current owner of ranch San Ignacio in Paso Robles, California, which used to belong to Maestro Paderewski.

When you enter the building, you will find yourself in a large rectangular hall. A portrait of Ignacy Jan Paderewski and a bronze bust of the Polish national poet Adam Mickiewicz by a renowned French sculptor and a friend of the poet Pierre Jean-David, greet the visitors introducing them to the Polish culture and history. The pieces of Polish art that the

Embassy is most proud of are on the second floor. Among the paintings hanging on the walls of the main salon the most interesting are: *The Hunt* by Julian Fałat and *The Fencer* by Jacek Malczewski. Both were painted at the turn of the 19th and 20th centuries and are among best examples of Polish painting of the period. Others include copies of the well-known *Court Jester* by Poland's most famous painter of the 19th century – Jan Matejko and a copy of a large oil painting of a great Polish 17th century military leader, Grand Crown Hetman Stefan Czarniecki by Brodero Matthisen (1659). Over the fireplace hangs a portrait of Prince Kazimierz Lubomirski (the Envoy who purchased the building) painted by Tadeusz Styka in 1921. The corner of the salon adjacent to the living room is devoted to Ignacy Jan Paderewski. The Steinway grand piano which stands there was donated to

The statue of Ignacy Jan Paderewski
on the Embassy grounds.
Photo by Richard Poremski.

The Blue Salon with the Dining Room in the background.
Photo by Mariusz Brymora.

Paderewski's grand piano and his portrait by M. Sancewicz in the Blue Salon
of the Embassy. Photo by Mariusz Brymora.

the Embassy by the Maestro himself. When in 1941 he fell ill and realized he would not be able to play any more, he gave the instrument to the Embassy, headed at that time by his long time co-worker – Jan Ciechanowski. Paderewski looks over the salon from his portrait by Maciej Sancewicz, which hangs above the piano.

From the Blue Salon, wide doors lead to a small hexagonal room which used to be called the Sitting Room. It is decorated with two 19th century portraits of women and an antique French bronze clock with cherubs. Other decorative elements include copies of the bronze busts of two American Founding Fathers: George Washington and Benjamin Franklin made by the French sculptor Jean-Antoine Houdon. Adjacent to the Sitting Room is the Fountain Room, named so because of the little fountain located opposite the entrance, decorated with a relief of a man's face looking from the overhead, and a semicircular back wall of mirrors which scatter the reflections of people standing in front of them.

Another important room on the main floor of the Embassy is the Great Ballroom lit by two 24-light brass chandeliers. The dominant decorative element of the ballroom is the mural called *The Glory of the Polish Arms*.

The Small Salon with the Fountain Room in the background.
Photo by Mariusz Brymora.

The Great Ballroom with The Glory of the Polish Arms mural.
Photo by Mariusz Brymora.

The painting depicts two key historical figures – Marshal Józef Piłsudski, the chief of the newly born state in the 1920s, on horseback of his beloved *Kasztanka* and King Jan III Sobieski remembered first of all for his triumphant victory over the Turks at Vienna in 1683. The work was created by Jan Henryk de Rosen[26] in 1938. As it fits so well into the wall of the ballroom it became known as a mural, even though it was actually painted on canvas. Many visitors to the Embassy may not remember seeing this piece of art in spite of its huge size. In 1947, the authorities decided that images depicting soldiers of the Legion's First Brigade, a banner with an icon of the Black Madonna of Częstochowa or the coat-of-arms of the Commonwealth of Poland and Lithuania on the shield carried by King Jan were not in line with the ideology of the socialist government. The mural was covered with plywood and disappeared from the ballroom's wall. Only after 40 years, it was

---

26 Jan Henryk de Rosen (1891–1982) – Polish artist, master of mural and mosaic works. He took active part in World War I, fighting in the French and the Polish Armies. He served as attaché and translator to I.J. Paderewski at the Versailles Peace Conference. In 1937, at the invitation of Ambassador J. Potocki, he travelled to the United States where he spent the rest of his life pursuing his artistic career. Apart from the painting at the Polish Embassy, his most renowned work is the critically acclaimed mosaic "Christ in Majesty" at the Basilica of the National Shrine of the Immaculate Conception in Washington D.C. At 3600 square feet and nearly 3 million tiles, it is one of the largest mosaics of Jesus in the world.

The Hunt by Julian Fałat (c.1890), the Blue Salon of the Embassy.
Photo by Gregory R. Staley. Source: Archives of the Polish Embassy in Washington.

The Fencer – self-portrait
by Jacek Malczewski (c. 1908);
the Blue Salon of the Embassy.
Photo by Mariusz Brymora.

"rediscovered" during the redecoration project of 1987. The workers took it down, cut it into six pieces (!) and sent them to Warsaw. It was only thanks to the artistry of the Polish restorers that the painting could be renovated and returned to the Embassy. Since 1995 it has been on show in its original place.

Two of many portraits displayed on the Embassy walls show the most famous Polish soldiers in America. One depicts Tadeusz Kosciuszko whose portrait is a copy of the famous oil by Josef Grassi. The other one is a portrait of Kazimierz Pulaski – another hero of the American Revolutionary War. Next to it stands a flagpole with a replica of the banner of Pulaski's Legion donated to the Embassy by The National Society of the Sons of the American Revolution.

This little collection of art together with the interior decorations of the building are responsible for the most common reaction of the American guests who – when entering the building for the first time – usually utter the most popular word of admiration – "WOW!". Stunned by its beauty, these people still do not realize how many famous political figures, artists and other guests have visited the Embassy over all those years and how many crucial historical events this place has silently witnessed.

The building of the Consular Division and Defense Attaché Office
in Wyoming Avenue, Washington D.C. Photo by Mariusz Brymora.

The current Ambassador's residence in Whitehaven Street,
off Massachusetts Avenue in Washington D.C. Photo by Mariusz Brymora.

The building in 16th Street is the place where the Chancery of the Embassy has been operating for a hundred years. It is not, however, the only location where the offices of the Embassy are situated. The Consular Division has its own premises at 2224 Wyoming Ave. This building also hosts the offices of the Polish Military and Naval Attaché. The Economic Division is located just off Dupont Circle, at 1503 21st Street.

In November 2008, Poland purchased the new Ambassador's Residence at a very prestigious location in Whitehaven Street, almost in the heart of Washington Embassy Row. It is another historical building, erected in 1927 for a renowned art collector and philanthropist Paul Mellon, which is a fine example of the Georgian style in American architecture. Adjacent to the British Embassy and located next door to the Washington home of the former U.S. President and Secretary of State, Bill and Hilary Clinton, the house is one of the finest amba-ssadorial residences in the city.

A few months after establishing the Polish Legation in Washington, on June 1, 1920, the Consulate General of Poland was founded in Chicago – the city which since the 19th century had been regarded as the capital of the American and world *Polonia*. At the request of its first Consul General Zygmunt Nowicki, the Consulate found its place at the offices of the Polish Women's Alliance of America at 1309 North Ashland Avenue, conveniently located in the heart of the so-called Polish Triangle where, at that time, a vast majority of Poles in Chicago resided. The location was inasmuch interesting as the genesis of this organization was strictly feminist. Women who were deprived of the right to membership in earlier fraternal organizations of Polish Americans decided to fight for their rights and founded their own organization in 1898. It was them who hosted the Polish Consulate and gave it its first address in the Windy City.

At that time, Pittsburgh and Buffalo were among the American cities with biggest Polish populations so the missions in these two cities were among the first consulates set up in the United States. On March 5, 1920, the Consulate in Pittsburgh was established (217 N. Craig Avenue) with Kazimierz Kurnikowski as its head. In the same year, Buffalo Consulate opened its premises at 761 Fillmore Avenue, and was headed by Consul Stanisław Manduk.

On March 22, 1921, the Polish Consulate in Detroit began its operation at 80 Garfield Avenue. It was headed by Consul Jerzy Barthel de Weydenthal whose jurisdiction covered the states of Michigan and Ohio. A few days before the inauguration, the Polish Daily, *Dziennik Polski*, published quite a detailed guide for the Consulate's petitioners describing the activities of the mission and giving them some good advice. One of the tips said:

"When presenting to the Consulate a request in writing one had to present the case clearly and succinctly describing all the circumstances which might be helpful to the official handling of the matter. One should bear in mind that too long a letter from one petitioner consumes time that officials might otherwise devote to handling cases brought by other petitioners."[27]

When applying for the Polish passport a person was required to file an application with four photographs and a fee of … 12.50 USD (just to satisfy the Reader's curiosity, the current fee is 132 USD).

The only Polish Vice Consulate (this category of mission was shortly given up) operated for a short time in St. Louis, MO. In April 1923, the

The Embassy building on one of these rare snowy mornings
in Washington D.C. Photo by Mariusz Brymora.

---

27 *Dziennik Polski*, March 17, 1921, p. 3. (the excerpt translated by M. Brymora).

President of Poland and the Minister of Foreign Affairs in their official letter nominated Władysław Kozłowski to be the Vice Consul there with a jurisdiction over a huge territory of seven states: Missouri, Kansas, New Mexico, Texas, Oklahoma, Arkansas and Louisiana.[28]

---

28 *Traditions of Polish Diplomacy 1918–1939*, Ministry of Foreign Affairs, Warsaw 2008, p. 106.

Into the Second Republic

Despite achieving great personal popularity, Lubomirski accomplished no spectacular successes of his campaign to secure American loans for Poland. Little engagement of the American government into the Polish–Soviet conflict and the Silesia cause ended in his resignation as early as in the summer of 1921. The following year (December 1922), he was replaced by Władysław Wróblewski who in turn was succeeded at the end of 1925 by Jan Ciechanowski, Paderewski's chief Secretary during Peace Conference in Paris in 1919.

For the first ten years of the presence of Polish diplomats in the U.S. capital the mission had remained just a Legation. In December 1929, Representative Hamilton Fish, Jr. introduced a resolution to the House in which he said:

"… there is no nation in Europe which has a more friendly and cordial feeling toward the United States than Poland for the aid given by the American delegates at the Peace Conference towards the establishment of the present Republic of Poland. (…) It is only fair and right that we should recognize the freedom and independence of the Polish people by exchanging Ambassadors with the present well-established and powerful Republic of Poland."[29]

In a secret report to the Ministry in Warsaw the *charge d'affaires* of the Polish Embassy informed the chief of the Polish diplomacy:

"One might add that on the 20th day of this month Congressman Fish and his wife were guests of Envoy Filipowicz at a dinner honoring the French Ambassador. It was on this very day that the House of Representatives passed the Embassy Act, accepting Fish's proposal. Mr. and Mrs. Fish wanted to be at the Polish Legation on that memorable

---

29 Statement of the Representative Hamilton Fish, Jr. in favor of the resolution which he introduced on December 2, 1929 to appoint an ambassador to the Republic of Poland. Source: Polish Embassy in Washington Archives, the Hoover Institution, Stanford University.

day so badly that Mrs. Fish, despite breaking an elbow a few hours earlier, attended with her arm in a plaster cast."[30]

The Legation was raised to Embassy level and on March 4, 1930, Tytus Filipowicz (the Envoy since March 1929) presented his credentials to President Hoover and became the first Polish Ambassador to the United States. Shortly before, on the last day of January, the American President nominated Alexander P. Moore to be the first Ambassador to Poland. Sadly, he died before he could assume the office and consequently John Willys was appointed to the post. By presenting his credentials on May 24, 1930, he became the first American Ambassador in Warsaw.

There is little if any doubt that one of the most interesting ambassadorships of the prewar period was that of Count Jerzy Potocki who

The first Ambassador of Poland to the United States – Tytus Filipowicz (in the middle) on the day of presenting his credentials to President Herbert Hoover in March 1930. Here with Captain Allen Buchanan (third from right) and Francis White (far right). Source: the National Digital Archives in Warsaw.	A shake hand of Ambassador Tytus Filipowicz (left) and Ambassador John Willys in 1930. Source: the National Digital Archives in Warsaw.

30 Secret report No 11/T/30 from January 30, 1930 (the excerpt translated by M. Brymora). Source: Polish Embassy in Washington Archives, the Hoover Institution, Stanford University.

Ambassador Tytus Filipowicz (second from the right) visiting
the Consulate General in Chicago in December 1931. On his right,
Consul General Tytus Zbyszewski. Source: the National Digital Archives in Warsaw.

became a symbol of the Polish diplomacy in Washington. A full-blooded
aristocrat, the heir to the magnificent palace in Łańcut (Poland), educated
at best European Universities, and a former Polish Senator he arrived in
New York on May 27, 1936 as one of the passengers of the maiden voyage
of *MS Batory*, the new Polish liner from Gdynia. His tenure in Washington
was the time when the Embassy became the place of thriving social life.
One of the most handsome and most popular diplomats in Washington,
whom the press called "a great favorite in Washington society," Count
Potocki gave numerous parties and receptions attended by all celebrities
(as we would call them today). He also invited to Washington the painter
Jan Henryk de Rosen who created *The Glory of the Polish Arms* – the mural
which still decorates the Great Ballroom of the Embassy (see p. 44).

Meanwhile, the Consulate in New York moved to the corner of Third Avenue
and East 57th Street. A rather amusing story happened there in December

1921, when the postman delivered three suspiciously looking packages addressed to Consul General Dr. Stefan Grotowski. The Polish officials feared a bomb attack and immediately called a bomb squad. When the head of the bomb unit opened the packages, he found half a million marks issued in Poland before the country regained independence. The money had been sent by Polish immigrants to be exchanged for a new issue of notes.

In spring 1929, the Polish Government purchased from the Neurological Institute the property at 149 East Sixty Seventh Street which was to host the Polish consular office for the next 25 years. A little later, on September 1, Mieczysław Marchlewski was appointed Consul General in New York. A terrifying moment occurred when they were moving offices. While removing a desk from the old office, a mover was wounded when a revolver in one of the drawers fired. Luckily, the wound in the chest was only a minor one. The weapon was the property of the Polish Consul.

In those old days, when the pace of life was much slower than it is today, the American press seemed to be interested in things that do not necessarily

Ignacy Jan Paderewski at the Consulate General of Poland in New York with Ambassador Tytus Filipowicz (left) and consul Mieczysław Marchlewski (right). Source: the National Digital Archives in Warsaw.

From the left: Consul General in New York
Lech Byszewski, Consul in Buffalo Stanisław Rosicki,
Consul in Pittsburgh Artur Ocetkiewicz (c. 1929–1931).
Source: the National Digital Archives in Warsaw.

catch so much attention of the mainstream media today. In November 1934, the reporter of *The Washington Post* who was covering the Polish Independence Day celebration included in his article a detailed description of the outfit of one the Polish host ladies:

"Nearby stood Mme. Sokolowska, wife of the Counselor of Embassy, wearing an afternoon gown fashioned of black taffeta with a long tunic of dark green crepe embroidered with gold. The skirt of the gown was ankle length and slashed to the knee in front of the latest Parisian manner. Her hat was of black velvet trimmed with paridise [original spelling – M.B.] tips."[31]

After only a few months, the Consulate in Chicago also had to find a bigger office and moved to its first independent location at 1115 North

---

31 *Polish Independence Day Celebrated at Embassy*, *The Washington Post*, November 12, 1934.

Damen Avenue where it remained nearly until the end of 1925. In the presence of Consul General Count Jerzy Barthel de Weydenthal, on November 8, 1923, crowds of Polish Americans gathered there to greet the Polish hero and commander – General Józef Haller[32] who came to America with a good will mission and while in Chicago, decorated his former soldiers with Crosses of Valor.

These early changes of address were only the beginning of the moves of the Polish Consulate in the Windy City which were to follow. For the next seven years it was located at the America Fore Building at 844 North Rush

General Józef Haller with Ambassador Władysław Wróblewski and a group of Polish and American officers during his visit to the United States in 1933.
Source: the National Digital Archives in Warsaw.

---

32 Józef Haller (1873–1960) – a Lieutenant General of the Polish army; he is most remembered for the creation (on behalf of the Polish National Committee) of what is known as Haller's Army or the Blue Army (from the color of its French uniforms). His army, formed in France in the summer of 1918, was allied with the Entente and fought against Germany for a few months.

Ambassador Jerzy Potocki with the Polish Minister of Industry and Commerce
Antoni Roman (in the middle) and Deputy Minister of Communication
Aleksander Bobkowski (far right) during their visit in Washington May 9, 1939.
Source: the National Digital Archives in Warsaw.

Street. From the fall of 1931 until the spring of 1935, it occupied the house
at 1555 North Dearborn Parkway and in April 1935, it moved to Lake
Shore Drive for the first time finding its location in an impressive building
at 1444 which used to be the residence of the Chicago banker George
Reynolds (the house was demolished at the beginning of the 1960s). The
Consulate stayed at this address until 1940 when, facing the war reality
and looking for reducing the costs, Consul Ripa terminated the lease
contract and moved the offices to Cedar Street.

Unfortunately, the promising years of the Second Republic during which
the Polish diplomatic activity started to enjoy its first successes, did not
last long. Less than twenty years after regaining independence, Poland
found itself on the verge of another devastating conflict. Soon Ambassador
Potocki had to face a serious task of informing the public about the

Opening of the Polish pavilion at the World Exhibit in New York in 1939.
Sitting in the car: Comissioner of the Exhibit Grover A. Whalen (second seat
on the left), Ambassador Jerzy Potocki (next to Whalen), Minister Antoni Roman
(behind the Ambassador). Source: the National Digital Archives in Warsaw.

Polish Ambassadors to the United States during the Second Republic:
Władysław Wróblewski (left), Stanisław Patek (midle), Jan Ciechanowski (right).
Source: the National Digital Archives in Warsaw.

The Consulate General at 1555 N. Dearborn Parkway in Chicago in 1932.
Source: the National Digital Archives in Warsaw.

The building at 1555 N. Dearborn Parkway –
contemporary view – the seat of the Consulate
General in Chicago from 1931 until 1934.
Photo by M. Brymora.

The building of the Consulate in Pittsburgh (undated, most probably from early 1930s). Source: the National Digital Archives in Warsaw.

The building of the Consulate General in Detroit (undated, most probably beginning of the 1930s). Source: the National Digital Archives in Warsaw.

The building of the Polish Consulate in Buffalo in 1932.
Source: the National Digital Archives in Warsaw.

situation in Europe and the position of the Polish Government when it became evident that war was only a matter of time. While officially opening the Polish Pavilion at the World Fair in New York on May 3, 1939, the day of Polish National Holiday,[33] the Ambassador, accompanied by the Consul General in New York Sylwester Gruszka and the Commissioner General of the Fair Baron Stefan de Ropp, declared that Poland would fight if invaded by Germany.

The War Turmoil

On the day of the outbreak of the war, September 1, 1939, Ambassador Potocki summoned Polish Consuls General from Chicago, New York and Pittsburgh to a meeting in Washington in response to reports of the German invasion of Poland. The following day, in his statement made on CBS Count Potocki assured that "Poland stands firm and shall fight back." He went on explaining:

> "We did not desire the war. We did everything in our power to prevent it. When the history of this crisis is written it will testify to the patience and determination of the Polish people to hold fast to peace in the face of provocation. We knew this attack would come but we refrained from the advantage of striking first. We may have lost military benefits, but we desire to stand clean before history."[34]

Just little over a fortnight later, Ambassador Potocki had to react to the aggression of the Soviets who stabbed Poland in the back by invading her territory from the East. On September 19, while addressing the conference of the World Federation of Polish Jews Abroad, he promised that "the time will come, as it has so often in the history of our country, that Poland will rise again." Even though Poland ceased to exist as a country, the American Administration never withdrew its recognition for our state. In the first days of October 1939, Secretary of State Cordell Hull announced on behalf of the American Government that "the United States continues to regard the government of Poland as in existence [following the outburst of the war the government fled to Paris and then to London where it remained for the duration of the war – M.B.], in accordance with the provisions of the Constitution of Poland, and continues to recognize Count George Potocki as its Ambassador in Washington."[35] The Embassy, to which thousands of

---

34 Quoted after *New York Times*, September 2, 1939.
35 *New York Times*, October 3, 1939.

volunteers reported, became a center of organizing aid for occupied Poland. All Polish diplomatic missions announced they would remain open "as usual" despite the outbreak of hostilities in Europe and hoping that the downfall of the Polish Republic is only temporary.

One of the last ambassadorial duties of Count Potocki was to greet Ignacy Jan Paderewski in New York harbor, who came to America one more time precisely on the day of his 80th birthday. This was already the time when rumors of Potocki's resignation were wide spread. Just a few days later, it was officially announced that his resignation was filed with the Government in Exile. The reason of it was not officially revealed, however, it was generally assumed that it was the publication by the Germans of the so-called "Potocki Papers," the alleged confidential reports to the Polish Government, in which Potocki was critical of the Roosevelt Administration, accusing the U.S. President of inciting war in Europe.

Ignacy Jan Paderewski greeted
in New York by the U.S. Ambassador to Poland
Anthony D. Biddle on November 6, 1940,
the day the great Pole celebrated his 80th birthday.
Source: the Paso Robles Paderewski Collection,
Polish Music Center, USC.

Many Washington diplomats, high rank representatives of the American administration and friends came to the Embassy on December 10, 1940 to attend the farewell party. *The Washington Post* called it "one of the outstanding events of the season" and "the final fling" of one of the most colorful figures among the pre-war diplomats.

In March 1941, the Embassy was taken over by Jan Ciechanowski for whom it was the second term as the Polish Envoy in the U.S. Previously he had served as the head of the Polish Legation from December 1925 until April 1929. This time Ciechanowski came to Washington from the post of the Deputy Foreign Minister of the Polish Government in London. When he met the President to present his credentials, Roosevelt showed his interest in the activity of the Polish Government in London and asked the Ambassador to arrange for the visit of its head to Washington. Shortly afterwards, the Prime Minister of the Polish Government in Exile and the Commander of the Polish Army, General Władysław Sikorski[36] came to America for a few weeks. In Washington, he conferred with President Roosevelt. During a press conference at the Embassy, Sikorski commented on his meeting with the President saying, "there is not a slightest doubt as to the President's very friendly attitude to Polish problems and his understanding of European problems." From Washington General Sikorski went to Palm Beach where he met with Ignacy Paderewski, and then to Chicago where he was received by Polish Consul General Dr. Karol Ripa at the new office of the Consulate at 49 E. Cedar Street. On April 20, 1941, a fine reception was held there in honor of General Władysław Sikorski, accompanied by Ambassador Ciechanowski and Stanisław Mikołajczyk.[37]

On June 29, 1941, at the Buckingham Hotel in the heart of Manhattan, almost opposite Carnegie Hall, died Ignacy Jan Paderewski – one of the

---

36 Władysław Sikorski (1881–1943) – Polish political leader and military man. After the outbreak of World War II he became the commander in chief of the Polish Armed Forces and the Prime Minister of the Government in Exile which was recognized by the western allies. In 1943, after visiting Polish forces stationed in the Middle East, the plane carrying General Sikorski and his companions crashed into the sea immediately after the takeoff from Gibraltar Airport killing all on board but the pilot.

37 Stanisław Mikołajczyk (1901–1966) – Polish politician, Prime Minister of the Polish Government in Exile during World War II, and Deputy Prime Minister in post-war Poland until 1947. He escaped to the United States after falsified elections in Poland in January 1947 and spent the rest of his life in Washington D.C.

General Władysław Sikorski at a meeting with Polish veterans during his visit
to the United States in 1942; to his right Ambassador Jan Ciechanowski.
Source: the National Digital Archives in Warsaw.

greatest Polish statesmen of all times. His body was taken to St. Patrick's
Cathedral where he lay in state and where a solemn pontifical mass of
requiem was celebrated by Archbishop Francis Spellman. The Polish
delegation was headed by Ambassador Ciechanowski. He and the Polish
Consuls General: Sylwester Gruszka from New York, Karol Ripa from
Chicago, and Heliodor Sztark from Pittsburgh were amongst the throngs
of official mourners which included diplomats representing many
countries, American public officials, musicians, and over 4500 Polish
and American fans and admirers who crowded in the Cathedral.
Additional 35,000 people stood outside and along the line of the funeral
procession to pay tribute. The body of the greatest pianist among Prime
Ministers and the greatest Prime Minister among pianists was carried on
a horse-drawn gun caisson, accompanied by a guard of honor, to
Pennsylvania Station from where it was taken by train to Washington.
The car in which the pianist had toured America rolled into the Union
Station shortly before six in the evening. The capital city welcomed the
Maestro for the last time to the sound of incessant thunder accompanied

by blinding lightening. The whole staff of the Embassy lined along the platform and the coffin was followed by a dozen of Polish veterans of World War I. The body was taken to the Embassy's ballroom where it lay in state. The door stayed open until 11 at night because, despite torrential rain, over 5,000 people, from ambassadors and government officials to anonymous music fans, came to visit and pay their last respects. The Undersecretary of State, Summer Welles, represented the American President, who sent a wreath of orange gladioli. The death of Paderewski was widely covered by the American press and it captured attention of the American society and authorities, becoming a great demonstration in honor of Poland. On Saturday, July 5, the body of Paderewski was taken to Arlington National Cemetery where a battery of cannon boomed a 19-gun salute in his honor and the U.S. Army Band played a funeral dirge before he was buried under the mast of the battleship *USS Maine*. It was the decision of President Roosevelt himself to grant permission to rest the mortal remains of Paderewski at Arlington (an honor normally reserved to American citizens only) with the assumption that they would stay there until the time when Poland is free again and the great Pole could return to his homeland. The time the President most probably had in mind was the end of WWII and surely no one at that moment did expect that it would take over 40 years to make Paderewski's comeback to free Poland possible. In 1992, Ambassador Kazimierz Dziewanowski worked with a special committee under General Edward Rowny[38] which arranged for the remains to be transferred to Warsaw. On June 29 that year, a special U.S. military plane flew the remains from Andrews Air Force Base near Washington to

---

38 Edward Rowny (1917–2017) – Polish American, U.S. Army Lieutenant General, a military advisor to five American presidents and chief negotiator on the Strategic Arms Reduction Treaty (START). In 1989, President Reagan awarded Ambassador Rowny the Presidential Citizens Medal. The citation read: "Edward L. Rowny has been one of the principal architects of America's policy of peace through strength. As an arms negotiator and as a presidential advisor, he served mightily, courageously, and nobly in the cause of peace and freedom." In 1992, Rowny fulfilled his ambition by heading the honorary committee which planned and carried out the return of Ignacy Jan Paderewski's remains to Poland. He continued to promote the legacy of Paderewski until the end of his long life through the Paderewski Scholarship Fund which he established in 2004.

Warsaw where on July 5, in the presence of Presidents Lech Wałęsa and George W.H. Bush, they were buried at St. John's Cathedral in the Old Town. Paderewski's heart, however, in compliance with his wish, remained in America and is encased inside a bronze carving in the shape of a spread eagle at the National Shrine of Our Lady of Częstochowa near Doylestown, Pennsylvania.

In 1943, Ambassador Ciechanowski hosted the famous Polish courier Jan Karski, who became known to the world as "the man who tried to stop the Holocaust." Karski witnessed unspeakable crimes against Jews in the Warsaw ghetto and a Nazi German death camp in Belzec where he was smuggled disguised as a Ukrainian guard. In 1942, he was sent by the Polish Resistance to the West to relate what he had seen. In Washington, Ambassador Ciechanowski arranged for him to meet with leading U.S. officials, including former President Herbert Hoover, Cordell Hull, Francis

The plaque at Arlington National Cemetery commemorating
Ignacy Jan Paderewski. Photo by Mariusz Brymora.

Biddle and finally with the Commander-in-chief, Franklin Roosevelt. Unfortunately, no one believed what Karski told them or – perhaps more likely – they were unable to comprehend what he was saying.

Yet another dramatic and historical moment Ambassador Ciechanowski had to take the Embassy through came at the end of the war. Having been nominated by President Władysław Raczkiewicz[39] and – in his deepest belief – representing the Polish Government in Exile, he was determined to do everything possible to keep the building of the Embassy secure and safe in the hands of the authorities in London which he considered the only legal government of Poland. He, like all other Polish ambassadors, was obliged to do so by the instructions prepared by the Polish Ministry of Foreign Affairs in London and distributed to all Polish diplomatic missions as early as on May 17, 1945. Hence, when towards the end of June 1945, he heard from the Polish Prime Minister that the withdrawal of recognition of the legal Polish Government by Britain and the United States was imminent, he decided to act. On July 3, 1945, by means of a transaction between him and the President of the newly established Polish American Congress[40] – Karol Rozmarek, the building was sold to the organization for 17,500 USD. On Thursday, July 5, the recognition of the "provisional Polish Government" by America became a fact. That evening, Ambassador Ciechanowski received an official note, signed by the Secretary of State, James F. Byrnes, which read:

"It is with great satisfaction that I announce that effective today as of 7:00 P.M. Eastern War Time the Government of the United States has established diplomatic relations with the newly formed Polish Provisional

39 Władysław Raczkiewicz (1885–1947) – Polish politician and diplomat, the first President of the Polish Government in Exile from 1939 until 1947. Until the recognition of the Warsaw Provisional Government in July 1945 he was recognized by the United States (and the world) as the Polish Head of State.
40 A huge congress of *Polonia* with over 2500 representatives of Polish community from across the United States met in Buffalo, New York, from May 28 to June 1, 1944. The gathering created the Polish American Congress which incorporated major Polish organizations in the United States. Karol Rozmarek of Chicago was elected its first President.

Government of National Unity now established in Warsaw. The establishment of this government is an important and positive step in fulfilling the decisions regarding Poland reached at Yalta and signed on February 11, 1945. (…) Mr. Arthur Bliss Lane,[41] whom I have chosen as United States Ambassador to Poland, will proceed to Warsaw as soon as possible, accompanied by his staff."[42]

Half an hour after receiving this note, Ciechanowski replied with his own note to Secretary Byrnes protesting against the decision of the American Government to recognize the new Polish government of Messiers Bierut[43] and Osóbka Morawski.[44]

"For the second time in history," he wrote in the note, "the Polish Nation is being deprived of its independence, though this time not as a result of events which took place in eastern Europe alone, but as a result of a war which the United Nations waged in the name of law and justice. Notwithstanding the recognition of this state of things by other States, the Polish Nation will never give up its right to an independent State, and for this right it will struggle unwaveringly."[45]

On the following day, news reporters were invited to the Embassy for the last press conference of Ambassador Ciechanowski. He handed them

---

41 Arthur Bliss Lane – Ambassador of the U.S. to Poland from 1944 until 1947. He was accredited to two Polish governments first to the Polish Government in Exile in London and then to the post-war communist government in Warsaw. In 1947, he resigned in protest to the falsified elections that were held by the Polish authorities. After returning to the United States, he wrote a book titled *I Saw Poland Betrayed* in which he revealed his opinion that the United States and Britain failed to keep their promise that the Poles would have free elections after the war.

42 Jan Ciechanowski, *Defeat in Victory*, Garden City, New York 1947, pp. 387–388.

43 Bolesław Bierut (1892–1956) – Polish communist activist and politician, Soviet NKVD agent; President of Poland from 1947 until 1952 and Prime Minster from 1952 until 1954. He died in rather mysterious circumstances during his trip to Moscow in March 1956, which gave way to speculations about poisoning or suicide.

44 Edward Osóbka – Morawski (1909–1997) – Polish communist politician. In June 1945, he was appointed Prime Minister of the Provisional Government of National Unity and remained in office until February 1947.

45 Jan Ciechanowski, *Defeat in Victory*, New York 1947, p. 393.

Ignacy Jan Paderewski meeting crowds of Polish veterans
in Oak Ridge, NJ on June 22, 1941, which turned out to be his last public
appearance. He is being kissed on his hand by one of the soldiers –
a sign of the highest possible respect in Poland.
Source: the Paso Robles Paderewski Collection,
Polish Music Center, USC.

copies of his protest and announced that rather than represent, even for a moment, an illegal communist government, he resigned from his functions as Polish Ambassador in Washington. The Embassy was locked and the keys were sent to the Department of State. By this symbolic gesture Ciechanowski avoided handing the building over to the communist regime. All five Polish Consulates were also closed at the request of the Ambassador and all their heads (Sylwin Strakacz in New York, Juliusz Szygowski in Chicago, Heliodor Sztark in Pittsburgh, Stanisław Angerman in Detroit, and Władysław Sokołowski in San Francisco) repudiated the new Provisional Government of National Unity in Warsaw. The

Department of State declared the Ciechanowski-Rozmarek transaction void and made the President of Polish American Congress sign the Quit Claim Deed in which he gave up all the rights to the building. The curtains were drawn at the windows of the Embassy, the consulates bore door signs "Closed," and Polish nationals in the U.S. found themselves without diplomatic and consular protection.

Ambassador Jan Ciechanowski leading the funeral procession
of I. J. Paderewski at Arlington National Cemetery on July 5th, 1941.
Source: Polish Embassy in Washington Archives, the Hoover Institution,
Stanford University.

Under the Communist Regime

For many years to follow the Embassy and the Consulates were to be boycotted by members of the Polish community in America. Traditional Pulaski Day Parade, held in New York since 1937 in honor of Kazimierz Pulaski, was turned into a demonstration against Warsaw Communist Government. Tens of thousands of Polish Americans protested under such slogans as "The Warsaw Puppet Regime Does Not Represent the Polish People" or "For Her Loyalty to the Cause of Freedom Poland Was Dismembered at Yalta." The vast majority of *Polonia* remained hostile towards the new representation of their homeland. It was acceptable to visit Polish Consulates for passport and other family reasons but maintaining social contacts was out of the question.

The only occasions when *Polonia* in bigger numbers came close to the buildings of Polish missions were the manifestations organized in protest against events in Poland.

Just a few days after the phony elections of January 1947, members of the Polish community in New York picketed the Consulate at 151 67th Street for many hours, protesting against falsification of the results by the communist party.

Chicago remembers the manifestation of a few thousand people in 1956 organized in protest against the riots in Poznań during which the regime troops brutally suppressed the protesting workers. Both the leaders of *Polonia* organizations (Karol Rozmarek and Roman Pucinski) and American politicians (Mayor of Chicago Richard Daley and Senator Paul Douglas) denounced these events in their passionate speeches.

The ban on Kazimierz Dejmek's production of *Forefathers' Eve* (Polish: *Dziady*) by Adam Mickiewicz at the National Theatre in Warsaw in 1968 brought angry crowds of Polish Americans to the front of the Embassy building. The students' protests in Poland (the so-called March events) followed by the anti-Semitic campaign of the communist government,

Polonia protesting in front of the building
of the Consulate General at 49 E. Cedar Street in Chicago.
Source: Wikipedia, public domain. Author unknown.
Published in *Dziennik Związkowy* on June 30, 1945.

as well as the participation of the Polish troops in the invasion of Czechoslovakia hampered the negotiations on Polish American Consular Convention. The document was eventually signed in 1972 as the first official agreement between the two countries regulating consular relations. Among other provisions, it guaranteed Polish citizens free contact with the consul and introduced an obligation on American authorities to notify the consul in case of a detention of a Polish citizen.

The peak of the anti-communist rallies came after the imposition of martial law in Poland in December 1981. The biggest pro-Solidarity demonstration took place in front of the Chicago Consulate on Lake Shore Drive at the very end of 1981 when the Polish American Congress and POMOST (Bridge) Foundation mobilized tens of thousands people to manifest their opposition to martial law and support for free trade union's demands.

Those who took part in these protests say that their only form of "contact" with representatives of the Polish authorities was when the latter ones peeped from the shut windows during the demonstrations to take pictures of those in front of the building.

* * *

Following the events of summer 1945, the war-time diplomats began to consider themselves refugees from the "new" Poland which was ruled by the authorities that were completely alien to them. It turned out that all members of the Polish consular and diplomatic corps started new lives in America, with the exception of one – a former financial counselor of the Embassy, Janusz Żółtowski, who took up his duties on behalf of the new Polish authorities as a newly appointed *charge d'affaires*. In September, he collected the keys to the Embassy from the Department of State and was supposed to represent the Polish authorities until a new ambassador was

Demonstration in front of the Embassy against the ban of Mickiewicz's *Forefathers' Eve* (*Dziady*) at the National Theatre in Warsaw in 1968. Source: private archives of Władysław Zachariasiewicz.

appointed. Żółtowski did fulfill his duties in an exemplary way until the summer of 1950 when he himself (as well as a number of other representatives of the communist regime) asked the American authorities for … a political asylum.

Just a few days before Christmas 1945, the office of the ambassador was taken by Oskar Lange who presented his credentials to President Harry Truman as the first Ambassador of the Polish People's Republic. He was a professor of Economics at the University of Chicago who came to the United States in 1937 and soon filed an application for the American citizenship. It was granted to him promptly and then became a major obstacle for him in becoming the Polish Ambassador. Even though Lange renounced his American citizenship, he was received by *Polonia* with great hostility. "Neither a Pole by origin, nor by belief" – shouted *Dziennik Chicagoski* – the main Polish language daily in those days. The Polish community in the U.S. became even more hostile towards the Warsaw regime authorities.

In the fall of 1945, all five of the Polish Consulates were taken over by the new regime. The circumstances which accompanied these acts were indeed very peculiar. The repudiation of the new Polish Government by the Ambassador and all Polish Consuls created a bizarre situation when the new authorities wanted to take over the Polish missions. There was no one there, all documents were either destroyed or deposited in a safe place (in case of Pittsburgh it is still not quite known what happened to them) and the new envoys had to use the assistance of the Americans to get into the buildings. The scenarios were identical at all Polish Consulates. In Detroit, for example, on November 10, 1945 at 11:00 a.m. a representative of the Department of State Mr. Albert Farmer met with the staff of the Polish Consulate headed by Consul Stanisław Angerman and took over from them all the documentation, money deposits and the rights to the building, for which he left a signed receipt. Fifteen minutes later, Olgierd Langer, an envoy of the Warsaw government, turned up at the Consulate to take the office from the Americans. A similar situation took place in San Francisco. When Consul Sokołowski refused to hand over the Consulate to a representative of the new government, he was notified by the Department of State that a Mr. Frank Paton would visit him to take over. Paton, in turn, passed it to Stefan Rogoziński who was sent from Chicago (which he had taken over a few weeks earlier) with an order to close the

Consulate down. Such acts, considered by *Polonia* as treason, were usually accompanied by protests of Polish Americans who would gather in front of the building where a new consul was installed, carrying banners with slogans like: "How does it feel to be a traitor?", "You have sold Poland. What are you doing here?" or "Down with the red fascists – Long Live Democracy!"

The controversy over the issue of recognition of one of the two existing Polish governments at that time (the London Government in Exile, not recognized by the Soviet Union and the Provisional Government of the Republic of Poland in Warsaw, not yet recognized by the Western nations) was responsible for Poland not being represented at the United Nations conference in San Francisco in the spring of 1945. In spite of all the behind the scenes negotiations of the world leaders, they could not break the deadlock over Polish representation. Maybe Poland lacked the statesman of the Paderewski caliber who could influence the decisions and developments. Nevertheless, it did have a special envoy in San Francisco who reminded over 3000 participants, including delegates and their advisors from 50 allied nations, UN staff and media representatives gathered at the War Memorial Opera House about the missing country. Arthur Rubinstein, a Polish artist of Jewish origin, one of the greatest pianists of the time, was to give a piano concert to entertain the guests. As usual, he was expected to start a wartime concert with the American anthem but when he noticed the absence of the Polish flag, he got furious and suddenly rose from the piano, asked everyone to stand up and played the Polish national anthem in support of the Polish cause. The event and Rubinstein's tribute to Poland hit the headlines in and outside California. Notwithstanding the absence of a delegate from Poland, the decision was taken to leave an empty space for the signature of a Polish representative under the text of the Charter of the United Nations. This way Poland became the founding member of the United Nations (the missing signature was placed under the document in October 1945 by Wincenty Rzymowski, the Foreign Minister of the new communist government).

The first Polish Envoy at the United Nations was Oskar Lange who for two years combined the duties in Washington and New York. Until 1959, the Polish Mission to the United Nations was located in the building occupied by the Consulate. Afterwards, it acquired its own seat at 9 East 66th Street in

Manhattan, in a building erected between 1909 and 1912 as the Charles and Louise Flagg Scribner, Jr. House. This location served as the Permanent Representation's office until 2011. Since then the Mission has been occupying two floors in one of the skyscrapers at the Grand Central Square.

During the first after-war years, the relations between Poland and the United States got very tense, especially after the elections of January 1947 which made the former Prime Minister Stanisław Mikołajczyk escape from Poland. The atmosphere was so bad that it could even result in breaking down the diplomatic relations. When President Truman received the new Ambassador, he told him bluntly that Warsaw violated its pledge to hold a free election. Nevertheless, he accepted the letters of credence of the new communist ambassador because, as he put it, "the Government of the United States has not lost interest in the welfare of the Polish people." Besides, the diplomatic ties were maintained only because the American Department of State came to the conclusion that their Embassy in Warsaw was in fact the only reliable source of information for them on what was going on in Poland and in the Warsaw Pact member states. With the appointment of Józef Winiewicz as the Ambassador, the Polish authorities hoped that this former member of Piłsudski's party and collaborator of the Ministry of Congress Works in Sikorski's government would regain for them the liking of Polish Americans and improve the relations with *Polonia*. Winiewicz was not lucky in fulfilling his task. He and Mikołajczyk, who escaped from Poland to the United States just a few weeks after Winiewicz had come to Washington, presented completely different reports on the recent general elections in Poland and as a result the Ambassador lost the last bits of rapport with Poles in America. Among Polish Americans who remembered his involvement with the London Government, Winiewicz gained an opinion of someone with the ability to position himself well with any ruling elite. Ciechanowski transformed himself into an unrestrained Ambassador, who fought against the New World Order. In May 1948 in Philadelphia, as a guest of the second Polish American Congress convention, he observed that:

> "Eleven nations, brutally seized by Moscow's totalitarian brand of communism and cut off from the West by the iron curtain – this is what constitutes today's reality; a terrible proof that Western statesmen

failed to keep their solemn promises that our mutual fight had one common goal, which was to establish the basic rules of the Atlantic Charter and the Four Freedoms across the world."[46]

Polonia, and oftentimes even the American Administration, did not treat the new Polish diplomats as their partners. They still recognized, at least unofficially, those who represented the Government in London. In October 1948, Polish Americans in Washington organized an event commemorating the anniversary of Pulaski's death. At the monument of the hero of the Revolutionary War in Pennsylvania Avenue the official guests included former ambassadors of the United States in Warsaw Arthur Bliss Lane and former Ambassador of Poland to the United States Jan Ciechanowski. The latter gave a very fervent speech in which he could not hide his indignation at the results of WWII for Poland as he believed that Poland was sacrificed by the wavering diplomacy of the Americans and the British, which yielded to the Soviets' imperialism and their territorial demands. "The world that was to be a one world, is torn into two," he thundered, "one suffering under the Soviet communist yoke, the other, still free, but fearful for its freedom."[47]

Ciechanowski remained very critical of America's role in arranging the post-war world deal and stood convinced that Poland was betrayed at Yalta when its main allies deserted his country and let the Soviet Union conquer it.[48]

The years following WWII was the time when Poland in fact had double diplomatic representation in the U.S. In 1951, Ambassador Józef Lipski (the pre-war Polish Ambassador to Germany) moved to Washington where until his sudden death in 1958, he was the official representative of the Polish Government in Exile. A vast majority of the Polish diaspora considered him the true envoy of the Polish authorities as opposed to the "regime ambassador" residing at 2640 16th Street.

---

46 Speech of Ambassador J. Ciechanowski at the second convention of Polish American Congress in Philadelphia on May 29, 1948 (the excerpt translated by M. Brymora). Source: Polish Embassy in Washington Archives, the Hoover Institution, Stanford University.

47 *Dziennik Chicagoski*, October 12, 1948.

48 Ciechanowski describes his feelings in his memories titled *Defeat in Victory* published by Doubleday & Co. in New York in 1947.

* * *

The 1950s brought many substantial changes on the Polish American diplomatic map. Firstly, the communist regime decided to close the Consulate in Pittsburgh. At the beginning of March 1950, yet another Polish diplomat resigned, this time Consul Józef Patyk in Pittsburgh. In his announcement he said he did it to protest against increased domination of Poland by the Soviet Union. Days later, it was announced that the Consulate would close on the last day of March because of "the reorganization of Polish consular offices in the United States." Zygmunt Fabisiak, the Polish Consul General in Chicago, followed in the footsteps of Mr. Patyk in August 1952 and sent an announcement of his resignation to the Department of State in Washington because he "couldn't stand the political situation in Poland." He added, "As Consul in Chicago I felt that I did not represent the real Polish interests" and asked for asylum for him and his family. Fabisiak was in fact the third consecutive Consul General in Chicago (after M. Cieplak and S. Rogoziński) who "chose freedom" and refused to obey decisions of the regime authorities. In August 1950, *The New York Times* published an article titled: *Three Polish Diplomats Ask Asylum Here; No 2 Man on Embassy Staff Is Among Them* and revealed in it that "the State Department estimated that the three new defections bring to twenty-five the number of Polish officials in this country who have broken with the Government since 1946."[49]

The escape of Gerhart Eisler, a Soviet spy organizing communist activity in America, on board of the Polish cruise liner *Batory*, the documentary evidence of the House Un-American Activities Committee claiming that the Polish Embassy in Washington was "a nest of spies," the activity of the Congress Katyn Commission[50] and its report as well as the

---

49 *The New York Times*, August 18, 1950.
50 In September 1951, the United States House of Representatives established the Select Committee to Conduct an Investigation and Study of the Facts, Evidence, and Circumstances of the Katyn Forest Massacre in which over 21 thousand of Polish officers and intelligentsia were executed in April and May 1940. Named the Madden Committee after its chairman, Rep. Ray J. Madden of Indiana, the committee assembled records relating to the massacre, in addition to hearing extensive witnesses' testimonies. The Madden Committee determined unanimously that the Soviet Secret Police (NKVD) was responsible for the executions and recommended a trial before the International World Court of Justice.

controversy over the Adam Mickiewicz Chair of Polish Culture at Columbia University were some of the events which made the Polish American relations more and more tense at the turn of the 1940s and the 1950s. In summer 1951, the Polish Government ordered the United States to close down its information service in Warsaw. In retaliation, the Department of State informed the Polish Ambassador that the Polish Research and Information Service in New York must be shut within 24 hours. The Cold War deepened and finally the State Department ordered that the Polish Consulates in Chicago, New York, and Detroit should be closed down. In the note delivered to the Polish Embassy on February 25, 1954, the Department of State said that the consular missions "serve no useful purpose in the conduct of relations between the United States and Poland" and that they should be closed "within reasonable time". On March 30, 1954, the Polish Consulate General at 1301 Richie Ct. in Chicago was closed down in response to the order from the State Department. Moving vans loaded with furniture and documents left for New York which was designated as the storage place. The New York Consulate also had to comply with the American decision, even though it shared the large seven – story building in East 67th Street with the headquarters of the Polish delegation to the United Nations which stayed in place. *Polonia* accepted the decision of the Department of State with no regrets. The Polish daily in Chicago wrote on February 27, 1954:

> "We bade farewell to our Comrade Consuls and their staff with no regrets because the consular missions were not Polish and their presence in our largest cities was redundant. Blindly obeying Moscow's orders, they did no business and had no petitioners, nor did they cover commercial interests, which were part of the consulate's portfolio. (…) These consulates had no contact with Polonia because Polish organizations, Polish American papers and our leaders did not maintain any relations with the people of the regime. (…) Let them go back to Bierut as neither we nor the Polish nation need them."[51]

After the Poznań riots of 1956 and the changes in Polish politics which followed, the icy atmosphere between the two countries grew slightly

---

51 *Dziennik Chicagoski*, February 27, 1954 (the excerpt translated by M. Brymora).

warmer. The thaw was made possible by growing economic cooperation (U.S. aid programs), cultural exchange (e.g. the 1958 tour of Dave Brubeck Quartet as goodwill ambassadors, which included twelve concerts in Poland) and bigger freedom of travel that Poles could enjoy (in 1958, the communist regime granted more passports to its citizens for travel to the United States and more visas for Americans to travel to Poland than in any year since the end of the war). After long negotiations, in the fall of 1958, the countries reached an agreement on reopening two Consulates: a Polish one in Chicago (with a jurisdiction on a huge territory of 28 states) and an American one in Poznań. That same year, the Polish Government bought a three-story residence at 1525 Astor Street to house its first Consulate outside Washington D.C. since 1954. When the Consulate was actually reopened in October 1959, major American dailies reported that Poland became the only country from behind the Iron Curtain to have a Consulate in the United States. New York still had to wait for quite a while before the Polish Consulate General was reestablished there in December 1972.

Despite the new developments, the attitude of the majority of the Polish diaspora to communist Poland did not change and the Polish American Congress officially announced the boycott of the regime Consulate in Chicago. The diplomatic relations between the two countries remained rather cold throughout the 1960s.

A rather unusual diplomatic incident occurred in 1966. It was the year when Poland celebrated a millennium of Christianity.[52] The Committee of Polish Americans set up in Buffalo successfully campaigned and made the U.S. Post Office issue a special postage stamp commemorating the occasion. However, a huge controversy aroused with an eagle – the symbol of Poland – at the heart of it. The bird appeared on the stamp wearing a crown surmounted by a Christian cross. The Polish authorities criticized the design because the eagle used in it was the pre-WW II symbol instead of the communist postwar eagle, which did not wear a crown. Despite official protests of the Embassy and the threat that Poland shall reject any

---

52 In 966, Duke Mieszko, the first ruler of the future Polish state, converted to Christianity and his personal baptism became known as the baptism of Poland which was a milestone in the Polish history with which Poland symbolically entered the Western Latin Civilization.

Members of the National Committee for the Millennium of Poland Stamp
during the unveiling of the design ceremony in the Postmaster General's
Reception Room in Washington D.C., June 1, 1966.
Source: private archives of Władysław Zachariasiewicz.

Honorable Lawrence F. O'Brien, Postmaster General, addresses Poland's Millennium
Stamp Dedication Banquet on July 30, 1966 at the Sheraton Park Hotel in Washington
D.C. Source: private archives of Władysław Zachariasiewicz.

mail bearing the five-cent commemorative stamp unless the bird is altered, the U.S. Post Office printed 115 million stamps with the Polish eagle wearing a crown underneath a Christian cross. An issuance banquet with over 1500 people in attendance was held in Washington D.C. on July 30 to celebrate the occasion.

* * *

The first half of the 1970s turned out to be the time of the greatest gains in Polish diplomatic properties in the USA. First, the Polish Government bought a new seat for the Consulate General in New York. On December 5, 1972, the Embassy, acting on behalf of the Polish People's Republic, bought the impressive De Lamar Mansion located in the very heart of Manhattan, on the corner of Madison Avenue and 37th Street. The price was 940,000 dollars and even though it must have seemed an enormous sum of money at that time it was a very good deal. Although very hard to estimate, the current value of the mansion is said to be close to one hundred million. The De Lamar Mansion is named after its first owner Joseph De Lamar. He was a Dutchman who, after spending his youth serving on ships, settled in Massachusetts. In 1870s, he struck it rich in the Colorado gold rush and within a few years made an astounding fortune estimated then at 20 million dollars. Towards the end of the 1880s, he settled in New York, started investing his wealth on Wall Street, got married, and tried to make social progress using his money. In 1902, the captain purchased a 50-by-100 foot plot of land in the heart of Murray Hill neighborhood paying 250,000 dollars and he commissioned a specialist in mansions C.P.H. Gilbert[53] to build him a house. The five-story mansion cost De Lamar about half a million dollars, it took three years to complete and became one of the most outstanding examples of Beaux-Arts architecture in New York.

---

53 C.P.H. Gilbert – Charles Pierrepont Henry Gilbert (1861–1952) was born in New York in a family which came to America from England two centuries earlier. He got his education in New York and in Paris. On his return from Europe, Gilbert settled in the West. He designed buildings in the mining towns of Colorado and Arizona but soon he moved back to New York and started designing buildings in Manhattan. In over 30 years starting from the mid-1880s, he designed more than 100 New York City mansions in various styles, with several significant buildings along Fifth Avenue. He was the architect of several important mansions on Fifth Avenue's "Millionaire Row."

The Consulate General of Poland in New York in 2002. Photo by Mariusz Brymora.

De Lamar lived in his residence only with his daughter Alice as he got divorced soon after contracting a marriage. After he had died of pneumonia in 1918, the residence was donated to the medical schools of Columbia, Harvard and Johns Hopkins Universities. Subsequently, it was sold to the American Bible Society in 1922. A year later, it was purchased by the National Democratic Club and became its seat for half a century. Since 1973, it has been serving as the Polish Consulate. The renovations performed on several occasions by Polish best specialists brought the mansion to its original beauty. The centennial anniversary of the building was the reason for weeklong festivities in October 2006, which became an impressive presentation of Polish culture and history. Well over a hundred years have passed since it was completed and the architecture style of the Big Apple has changed entirely, but the De Lamar Mansion remains one of the eye-poppers of Manhattan even today.

In a special publication celebrating the centennial of the building in 2006 titled *De Lamar Mansion. The Residence of the Consulate General of Poland in New York,* its author Michał Wiśniewski gives the following description of the architecture of the building:

The interior of The De Lamar Mansion – contemporary view. Photo by Mariusz Brymora.

"The main façade of the De Lamar Mansion and its entrance face 37th Street. The façade composition is dominated by a vertical tripartite division emphasized by side pavilions. (…) Most windows on the first three floors are paired and rectangular except for the single windows of the recessed rear part of the Madison Avenue façade. (…) The De Lamar Mansion is crowned above the third floor with a wide, detailed cornice carried on a massive paired console brackets at the corners and box brackets between. The corner pavilions flank the recessed and richly decorated central part, which is the most important element on the main façade composition. The double oak doors of the entrance are surrounded by a complicated composition of marble Ionic columns that support an ornamented lintel crowned with a decorated urn and cherubs, resting above a folate cartouche. (…) The entrance doorway is crowned with a stone balcony supported by console brackets. The balcony is composed as a decorative parapet with an elliptically arched window at the piano nobile. It is also decorated with stone openwork French doors, a wide volute frame and flanked with two thin, tall

The main salon of the Consulate building today. Photo by Mariusz Brymora.

rectangular side windows. The elegantly carved brackets and the keystone at the window arch support a handsome wrought – iron balcony at the third floor with a paired port-fenetre, flanked by thin side windows. The De Lamar Mansion is crowned with an ornamental wide cornice and tall mansard roof with dormers lighting the fourth and fifth floors. (…) The interiors represent Beaux-Arts flamboyance full of marbled and gilded ornaments. The building is organized around the oval staircase that is lit with a decorative skylight. On the first floor, apart from a large vestibule, there was a library and a billiard room to the west and a dining room and a service pantry to the east. The main kitchen of the building was originally located in the spacious basement, being connected with entire building by an additional staircase and an elevator. The piano nobile housed the ballroom and the neo-Pompeian room, which was De Lamar's private art gallery and was ornamented with Tiffany stained glass and well-known sculpture of *The Greek Slave* by Hiram Power. The gallery also housed a large collection of contemporary paintings, including well-known picture of *Aurore* painted by the French

Beaux-Arts master, Adolphe-William Bouguereau. The interior extension of the gallery was decorated with impressive mural paintings. They were completed by the mural painter and interior decorator active those days in United States Louis Schaettle. (…) For De Lamar's neo-Pompeian room Schaettle designed several murals of ancient subjects, including *A Tale of the Iliad* and *Ulysses Defying Circe.* The ballroom on the other side of the piano nobile was decorated with a large ceiling mural called *Passing of the Seasons*. The ballroom and the gallery were linked by a large hall with a musician's balcony on a mezzanine accessible from the main staircase."[54]

The latest addition to the site of the Consulate is a little monument erected in November 2007 in front of the entrance from 37th Street. It depicts Jan Karski sitting on a bench and playing a game of chess (the favorite pastime of the famous wartime courier).

It is difficult to imagine a better location for a consular mission in the Windy City than the one occupied by the Polish Consulate. Since 1974, the

Karski's bench in front of the Consulate General
of Poland in New York erected in 2007.
Photo by Mariusz Brymora.

54 *De Lamar Mansion. The Residence of the Consulate General of Poland in New York* by Michał Wiśniewski, New York 2006, pp. 28–31.

The Consulate General of Poland on Lake Shore Drive in Chicago in July 2001.
Photo by Mariusz Brymora.

Polish flag has been flying in front of the building at 1530 North Lake
Shore Drive, at the edge of the "golden mile." It is right in the center of the
Gold Coast – one of the wealthiest and most attractive neighborhoods in
Chicago. It was just an average and unexceptional district of the city until
1885, i.e. until when Potter Palmer, a Chicago prominent businessman,
built there the biggest private mansion in town, which looked like a little
castle. Over the following years, the Chicago elite gradually moved to this
area making it one of the most expensive realty districts in the whole of the
United States (zip code 60610).

Erected in 1916 as a private residence of a Chicago manufacturer
Bernard A. Eckhart, the building of the Consulate is one of the finest
examples of great mansions built at the turn of the 19th and 20th centuries
along Lake Shore Drive. It was designed by Marshal and Fox architectural
company, the same which built the Drake Hotel – one of the architectural
icons of the Windy City. The Polish Government bought the mansion in
1974 and moved the Consulate there from the adjacent Astor Street.

In *The Outline History of Polish Consulate General in Chicago* Steven
Monz gives the following description of the original building:

"The Bernard Albert Eckhart Mansion is considered an English town house with elements from the Italian Renaissance and is not tied to any historical prototype. The opulent limestone exterior has Italianate features, including two grand Palladian windows on the front or east façade and a three-arched loggia on the south. The most elaborate decor is found on the second floor, which has the character of the piano nobile of a Venetian palazzo. (…) Balustrades and sculpted frieze add visual interest here and throughout the façade. Pediments are over the third floor windows and an exquisite frieze surrounds the windows on the fourth floor. (…) Guests would gather in a large stairway hall and then (…) ascend to the second floor's piano nobile via a wide marble stairway with a beautifully carved balustrade or an elevator, both of which service all four floors. Arriving on this next level one had access either to the grand living room facing east, with a fireplace and a view of Lake Michigan; a palm room or solarium with a fountain and large windows to both the east and south; or to spacious formal dining room with south and west exposures. Also on this floor were the butler's pantry, kitchen servants' dining room, and access to the rear service stairway. (…) The third level was devoted to family use and had two bedroom suites for Mr. and Mrs. Eckhart, a guest bedroom suite, and a richly paneled library. The fourth level had three additional family bedrooms and several servants' areas."[55]

Although the building remained so attractive that it has all the time been the object of envy of consuls representing other Chicago consulates, it started showing more and more signs of wear and finally desperately needed a major remodeling. After many years of planning, the renovation started in the summer of 2006 and took almost two years to complete. Not only was the remodeling of the original building performed but also a brand new part of 4400 square feet was added to the structure and it houses most of the offices at present. The front part of the original building serves representation purposes and a modern customer service

---

55 *Outline History of Polish Consulate General in Chicago*, edited by Mariusz Gbiorczyk, Chicago 2010, pp. 43–44.

The building at 49 E. Cedar Street – contemporary view –
the seat of the Consulate General in Chicago from 1940 until 1948.
Photo by Mariusz Brymora.

1525 N. Astor Street – contemporary
view – the seat of the Consulate General
in Chicago from 1959 until 1974.
Photo by Mariusz Brymora.

hall is located there, too. The building was officially reopened on September 8, 2008 by the then Minister of Foreign Affairs Radosław Sikorski. It continues to make the Polish community proud of having its Consulate in such an impressive building in the heart of Chicago Gold Coast.

* * *

In 1972, Poland bought a big plot of land in Washington to build a new chancery there. A year later, the then Ambassador Witold Trąmpczyński officially said that Poland was planning to build a new Embassy in Tilden Street. About the location at 2640 16ᵗʰ Street he said, "The building is old and not really suitable for offices." The plans of the new building were sent to Warsaw where they came to the desk of Romuald Spasowski, the Deputy Minister who had previously served as the Polish Ambassador in Washington. Spasowski is said to have written on the proposal, "No, never, over my dead body". One could claim that his objection was so strong that it remained in power forever as the official seat of the Embassy has never changed.

Before he shocked the world with his famous defection after the imposition of martial law, Ambassador Romuald Spasowski had spent almost 10 years in Washington. This son of a Marxist professor, a devoted communist went through all stages of the diplomatic career. For the first time, he was appointed Ambassador to the United States in 1955 and stayed in office until June 1961. He was then replaced by Edward Drożniak, the only one among Polish ambassadors to the United States who died while in office (he suffered heart attack in 1966). Spasowski came to America again in 1978. Whereas his first ambassadorial tenure passed without too many extraordinary events, his second term of office was the time in Poland, which gave birth to Solidarity – the first independent Trade Union in this part of the world. After Solidarity was born, Spasowski started to show more and more sympathy for the new developments in Poland. Eventually, there were growing rumors that he was about to be called back as he no longer was a trusted member of the regime.

The double diplomatic life of an ambassador from those days can be seen in situations such as the dinner at the White House to which President Ronald Reagan invited Washington ambassadors in January 1981.

Spasowski provided two completely different accounts of the situation. In the report to Warsaw he wrote that:

"The United States traditionally have feelings of friendship towards Poland. [Reagan] himself as well as the government and the American nation follow closely the events in Poland. They pay special attention to bilateral relations and show kind attitude towards our affairs."[56]

In his memories titled *The Liberation of One*, which he published in America a few years after his defection, Spasowski described the very same meeting, saying:

"On January 27 President Reagan held a banquet for all ambassadors. [...] As Wanda and I were introduced, she hung back to allow me a moment with him alone. "Mr. President," I said, "Poland and the United States are connected by a long tradition of friendship. Now my country is in danger. I am asking you to support and to aid the Polish people. We Poles are counting on the United States."[57]

Before his superiors could actually call Mr. Spasowski back, martial law was introduced in Poland, which brought about his ultimate decision. On Saturday afternoon, December 19, 1981, the Ambassador picked up the phone and called Jack Scanlan, the Deputy Assistant Secretary for Eastern Europe. He told him he wanted to ask the President for a political asylum for him and his family thus becoming the highest Polish diplomat to have defected to the United States and the highest-ranking Communist diplomat to have done it throughout the entire Cold War. Within hours, he received a message that asylum had been granted and on that same evening a few CIA trucks came to the Polish residence in Albemarle Street in Forest Hills and took the Spasowskis and their belongings to a secret location. The following day at a crowded conference room of the Department of State, filled in with journalists from all over the world, Spasowski made his public statement which came to Poland as a complete shock when

---

56 AMSZ, Z. 50/84. T. AP.0-22, W 1; in Longin Pastusiak, *400 lat stosunków polsko--amerykańskich*, Warsaw, 2010 (the excerpt translated by M. Brymora).
57 Romuald Spasowski, *The Liberation of One*, San Diego 1986, p. 638.

broadcasted by Radio Free Europe and Voice of America. Within two days, Mr. Spasowski and his wife were at the Oval Office and hosted by President Reagan. It was at the end of this meeting when the famous picture was taken by a White House photographer showing President Reagan walking them personally to the car in drizzling rain and holding an umbrella over the three of them. The picture, likewise the decision and the statement of the Ambassador, became front-page news. Polish communist authorities sentenced him to death *in absentia* and deprived him of Polish citizenship. Even though he was fully rehabilitated in 1990, Spasowski never returned to Poland and died of cancer in Oakton, VA in 1995.

Following the imposition of martial law and the defection of the Ambassador, the Polish Embassy went quiet again. All social functions were suspended. The street in front of the Embassy became the place of frequent protests of the Polish American community of Washington area that would go there to burn Soviet flags and shout slogans against martial law rules back home. The Polish community wanted to stay as far away from the Embassy as they could. They stopped inviting Polish representatives to all their functions and did not want to be invited to the Embassy, which they would boycott for years to come.

In reaction to the Polish regulations of martial law, the Department of State decided to confine Polish diplomats to the cities where they were assigned, restricting their freedom of movement and travel guaranteed by the Vienna Diplomatic and Consular Conventions.[58] This was actually the second time of such restrictions because during the Cold War the U.S. government introduced similar curbing on the movement of communist countries diplomats (including Poland) which lasted from 1963 until 1974.

Despite some efforts to improve the mutual relations, they remained badly strained for a few years after Solidarity had been suppressed. In May 1982, the Polish government expelled two American Embassy officials. In retaliation, the U.S. ordered two Polish diplomats out of the country and suspended travel between the two countries for scientists taking part in

---

58 The Vienna Convention on Diplomatic Relations (1961) and The Vienna Convention on Consular Relations (1963) – international treaties which define a framework for diplomatic and consular relations between states and – among other things – guarantee things like immunity, freedom of movement or freedom of communication to all members of foreign missions in a receiving state.

research programs. In February 1985, the American military attaché and his wife were expelled from Poland because he was caught taking photographs of military objects and consequently accused of spying. The Department of State replied with expelling the Polish military attaché in Washington. In May of the same year, the U.S. government ordered four Polish diplomats from Washington and Chicago to leave the country in retaliation for the ousting of two officers of the American Consulate in Kraków who had been expelled from Poland earlier that month after having been accused of stirring anti-government demonstrations of young people in Kraków.

After the defection of Spasowski, the communist authorities did not send a new ambassador to the U.S. perhaps fearing that the Reagan Administration, which had imposed sanctions against Poland, would reject the appointment. No earlier than during the 1987 visit to Poland of the American Vice President George W. Bush was the decision announced that the two countries would exchange ambassadors again.

Ambassador Spasowski and his wife meeting President Ronald Reagan
at the White House on December 22, 1981.
Source: private archives of Wanda Spasowski.

President Ronald Reagan walking off
Ambassador R. Spasowski and his wife Wanda after
their meeting at the White House on December 22, 1981.
Source: private archives of Wanda Spasowski

The New Beginning

As a result of the activity of the Solidarity Trade Union and the Round Table talks, a partly free parliamentary election was held in Poland on June 4, 1989. Poles abroad were eligible to vote and thousands of people enthusiastically queued for hours in front of the Polish Embassy and especially the Consulates in Chicago and New York to cast their absentee ballots. The turnout was so big that the last votes were cast after midnight. Solidarity candidates gained an overwhelming victory and the first non-communist government since the end of WWII was formed under Prime Minister Tadeusz Mazowiecki. A short time later, in the fall of 1990, noncommunist diplomats took over the missions in the United States – Consul Hubert Romanowski started his tenure in Chicago and Consul Jerzy Surdykowski in New York.

A few months after the Berlin Wall had fallen, in July 1990, Kazimierz Dziewanowski came to Washington and introduced himself as the Ambassador of democratic and free Poland. His first open meeting at the Embassy attracted so many people that it had to be held outside of the building. Even though invitations had been sent out, virtually everyone who wanted to attend came to the Embassy. The crowd of a few hundred people enthusiastically received the man who after 45 years opened the Embassy door to them again. One of the leaders of the Polish diaspora commented on the event saying: "How different this is from two years ago when at the meeting with the folk ensemble 'Mazowsze' the presence of the Polish Consul was ignored both by the artists and the hosts."

Ambassador Dziewanowski, in turn, recollects the occasion in his memories when saying:

"We started with inviting the Washington Polonia to kind of 'opening of the Embassy.' The event was a great success; all the important individuals of Polish descent from Washington, Baltimore, Philadelphia and further neighborhoods attended, including many who have never been to the Polish Embassy. We somehow tried to control the number of guests, assuming that many people living farther away would be invited on another occasion, but we were not very successful. Everybody requested an invitation, we were embarrassed to refuse and as a result the number of guests several times exceeded that originally planned. The place was extremely crowded. The atmosphere was very moving. For many people this was the day of an ultimate breakthrough and re-establishing relations with their homeland. Many elderly people told me with affection about the day when the Embassy of their legitimate government in London was closed down, adding that following it they have never been to 16th Street again."[59]

Similar events followed in all other Polish missions and gave beginning to a new opening of the relations between Poland and her diaspora in America.

Even before the appointment of the new ambassador, just a few days after the actual fall of the Berlin Wall, the legendary leader of Solidarity, Lech Wałęsa paid his first visit to the United States. At the White House, President Bush called him "the spiritual godfather of a new generation of democracy" and bestowed upon him the Medal of Freedom – the highest civilian recognition one can be awarded by the United States. On November 15, 1989, Wałęsa made his historical address at the joint session of the American Congress as the third individual in history who, not being a head of state, had a chance to speak to the members of the whole Congress. His speech started with the magical words for the Americans "We the people" which gained Wałęsa the appreciation and friendliness of the audience since the very first minute of the address. Never in the past have so many people gathered at the Polish Embassy than during the evening reception to honor the Polish hero. It is said that over 600 people packed into the building. It was a challenge not only for the staff of the Embassy but also for the building itself. The lights were in full operation and at a certain moment all the light went out. The system turned out to be too weak and the overloaded fuses

---

59 Kazimierz Dziewanowski, *Polityka w sercu Europy*, Warsaw, 1995 (the excerpt translated by M. Brymora).

Ambassador Kazimierz Dziewanowski greeting Jan Nowak Jeziorański (top)
Edward Rowny (bottom left) and Jan Karski (bottom right) at Embassy events
in 1993. Photos by Albert Mogzec.

Lech Wałęsa signing the famous Gary Cooper Solidarity poster from 1989
during the Testimonial Dinner organized for him by American Center of Polish Culture
in Washington on September 15, 2000. The special version of the poster prepared
for this occasion by ACPC had Wałęsa's head in place of the head of Gary Cooper.
Photo by Albert Mogzec.

had blown. "Is there an electrician here?" someone shouted from the crowd. A loud burst of laugher went through the rooms of the Embassy making this an even more unforgettable evening for the gathered guests.[60]

Another occasion which proved that new times have come was the visit at the Embassy of Colonel Ryszard Kukliński[61] – "the first Polish officer in

---

60 Lech Wałęsa had worked as an electrician before he became the leader of Solidarity.
61 Ryszard Kukliński (1930–2004) – code name Jack Strong – a Polish officer and a C.I.A. spy who worked with the Americans for nine years providing them with Soviet military secrets including their plans to invade Poland in order to suppress Solidarity. He also gave advanced warning about Poland's plan to impose martial law. Facing imminent danger of being uncovered, he and his family were taken out of Poland by the C.I.A. in the fall of 1981. He was sentenced to death *in absentia* by a Polish military court. In the 1990s, both his sons lost their lives in unclear circumstances. In 1998, he was rehabilitated, restored to the rank of a Colonel and

NATO" as he was called by Zbigniew Brzezinski.[62] On February 28, 1998, at a festive event Colonel Kukliński was presented with a Certificate of, Appreciation by the Polish American Congress in recognition of his services to Poland. Among very few open meetings with *Polonia* which Colonel Kukliński attended, the one at *Dom Podhalan* in Chicago (the official seat of Polish Highlanders Association) is especially worth mentioning. On that evening, he appeared with two Russian dissidents Vladimir Bukovski and Viktor Suvorov (born Vladimir Bogdanovich Rezun) as well as the Polish journalist and activist, author of several books on Kukliński and his story – Józef Szaniawski. Chicago *Polonia* awarded the colonel with a replica of the shield of Hetman Stanisław Żółkiewski, Polish military commander of the Polish–Lithuanian Commonwealth, which symbolizes bravery and courage.

* * *

The great transformation of 1989 has brought one major change for the Polish diplomats serving in the U.S. After the long years of Cold War they at last could forget the famous *bon mot* of the British diplomat Henry Wotton who at the beginning of the 17th century said that "an ambassador is an honest man sent abroad to lie and intrigue for the benefit of his country." Their task was no longer to falsify the image of the country; on the contrary, the aim was to tell the Americans the true story of Poland's history, needs and goals. The new authorities considered the United States Poland's strategic partner and consequently the relationship with Washington became one of the priorities of Polish foreign policy. At that time, the most important task for Polish diplomats was to convince

---

posthumously promoted to Brigadier General. He died in Florida in February 2004 and a few months later his remains were transported to Poland and buried in the row of honor at Powązki Military Cemetery in Warsaw.

62 Zbigniew "Zbig" Brzezinski (1928–2017) – Polish American diplomat and political scientist. He was President Jimmy Carter's National Security Advisor from 1977 to 1981 and earlier served as a counselor to President Lyndon B. Johnson from 1966 to 1968. He was awarded Presidential Medal of Freedom for "his role in the normalization of the U.S. – Chinese relations and for his contributions to human rights and national security policies of the United States." He was on the faculties of Harvard, Columbia and Johns Hopkins Universities as one of the most renowned experts on international affairs.

Colonel Ryszard Kukliński with a certificate of appreciation presented to him by Polish American Congress at the Embassy of Poland on February 28, 1998. Behind him from left: Andrzej Jaroszyński (DCM), Ambassador and Mrs. Jerzy Koźmiński, Paul Sosnowski and Ted Mirecki (from Polish American Congress). Photo by Albert Mogzec.

Colonel Ryszard Kukliński, Polish Consul in Chicago Mariusz Brymora, Polish veteran Władysław Lis, President of Polish Highlanders Association – Henryk Mikołajczyk, and Józef Szaniawski – dissident, journalist and author of books on Colonel Kukliński at the meeting at *Dom Podhalan* in Chicago. Source: private archives of Mariusz Brymora.

American authorities that Poland's aspirations to become a member of NATO were justified and legitimate. Initially, the support for Poland's admission to NATO was built by Ambassador Dziewanowski. In June 1994, Jerzy Kozmiński took the office of Polish Ambassador and stayed in it for over 6 years supervising the Polish lobbying for NATO accession. He and his staff worked hard to persuade the American decision makers that the Pact's boundaries should be moved further east. All the diplomatic efforts, strongly backed by leaders like Jan Nowak Jeziorański,[63] Zbigniew Brzezinski (see footnote no 60) and the whole *Polonia* which united in this matter in an unprecedented way, were crowned on March 12, 1999 in Independence, Missouri when the Polish Minister of Foreign Affairs Bronisław Geremek and the American Secretary of State Madeleine Albright signed the documents at the ceremony of the deposition of Protocols of Accession. The Polish Minster noted in his address, "This is a great day for Poland, as well as for millions of Poles scattered all over the World. Poland forever returns where she has always belonged – to the free World. Poland is no longer alone in the defense of her freedom. We are in NATO 'for your freedom and ours'."[64] To Harry Truman Presidential Library which hosted the meeting he offered a copy of the poster of 1989 elections with a picture of Gary Cooper from the film *High Noon*. "It helped us to win," said the Minister. "For the people of Poland, high noon comes today."

---

63 Jan Nowak Jeziorański (1914–2005) – Polish journalist, writer and politician; the legendary courier from Warsaw, by many considered the greatest ambassador (not being a career diplomat) of Poland in the United States since Paderewski. He was born Zdzisław Antoni Jeziorański but used a number of *noms de guerre* during WWII, the best known of which was Jan Nowak which later became part of his original surname. During the war, he served as an envoy between the commanders of the Home Army and the Polish Government in Exile. He was the first to report to the West on the Warsaw Ghetto Uprising. Later he took active part in the Warsaw Uprising and eventually was sent as a courier to London again. He managed to bring to London a large quantity of documents and photos from the Uprising. After the war, Jan Nowak Jeziorański stayed in the West. From 1952 until 1976, he was the head of the Polish section of Radio Free Europe. After resigning from the post, he settled in the USA and became one of the most prominent members of the Polish American Congress. He also worked as an advisor to the American National Security Agency and Presidents Ronald Reagan and Jimmy Carter. He was an active supporter of Poland's entry into NATO and the European Union.

64 Bronisław Geremek's address at the ceremony of deposition of Protocols of Accession in Independence, MO on March 12, 1999.

Polish Minister of Foreign Affairs Bronisław Geremek and prof. Zbigniew Brzezinski in conversation with Ambassador Jerzy Koźmiński at the Embassy of Poland in Washington in February 1998. Photo by Albert Mogzec.

Foreign Minister Bronisław Geremek receives special edition of *Dziennik Związkowy*, Chicago Polish Daily, describing Poland's route to NATO from Les Kuczynski, National Executive Director of the Polish National Congress. Photo: Piotr Domaradzki. Source: Archives of *Dziennik Związkowy*.

Ambassador Przemysław Grudziński (in office from 2000 until 2005) had to face the implementation of NATO enlargement decision and as the Polish Ambassador witnessed another historical enlargement, this time that of the European Union which on May 1, 2004 accepted Poland and nine other new members. Poland's accession was preceded by a referendum in which Polish citizens, home and abroad, were voting whether to join the Union or not. Both the Embassy and the Polish Consulates all over America worked hard to convince *Polonia* that joining EU was a good thing for their homeland and that it did not threaten its sovereignty (which was a very popular belief among some Polish Americans). After a very exciting and tough campaign, which the Polish missions conducted for a few months, it was by a very small margin of a few hundred votes that Chicago saved itself from becoming the only "Polish" metropolis which would vote against Poland joining the European structures.

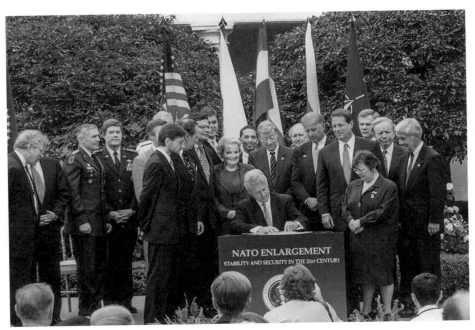

President Bill Clinton with highest representatives of his administration and Ambassadors of Poland, Hungary and the Czech Republic, signing the instruments of ratification for enlargement of NATO; White House, Rose Garden, May 21, 1998. Photo by Albert Mogzec.

Deputy Secretary of State Strobe Talbott speaking at the Embassy of Poland on
April 30, 1998, i.e. the day when the U.S. Senate voted to admit Poland, Hungary
and the Czech Republic into NATO. Standing next to him are Ambassadors:
Jerzy Kozmiński (Poland), György Bánlaki (Hungary) and Alexandr Vondra
(the Czech Republic). Photo by Albert Mogzec.

The day after the official admission of Poland to the European Union
family, Ambassador Grudziński wrote in his letter:
"The largest enlargement in the EU history is a complementary process
to the latest wave of the enlargement of NATO. The convergence of both
conforms the strategic direction of the Europeans – our desire to widen
a space of security and peace. (…) As a new element in the EU structure
my country will spare no efforts to improve the quality of transatlantic
relations, strongly believing that this is a key to peace and stability."[65]

Undoubtedly, Poland has kept the promise of her Ambassador.

The tenures of Ambassadors Janusz Reiter, Robert Kupiecki and Ryszard
Schnepf were the busy time of strengthening the relations between the two

---

65 Przemysław Grudziński, *Reborn Europe. A Stronger Partner, A Closer Friend, The Polish
Embassy Post,* No 14, Summer 2004, p.1.

Polish Minister of Foreign Affairs Władysław Bartoszewski addressing guests at the Embassy in April 2001 during the campaign for the EU accession. With him are Ambassador Przemysław Grudziński (on the left) and Jan Nowak Jeziorański (on the right). Photo by Albert Mogzec.

countries and developing the bilateral engagement between them in areas such as counter-terrorism, non-proliferation, missile defense, human rights, energy security and others. Gradually, Poland became considered one of the key U.S. allies and one of its strongest partners in Europe. One could claim that it was the time when President Bush's remark, made at The Wawel Royal Castle in Kraków in May 2003, that "Poland is a good citizen of Europe and Poland is a close friend of America – and there is no conflict between the two" found its full realization.

* * *

The post-1989 peaceful life of the Polish missions in America, filled in with busy consular and diplomatic activity was regrettably brutally interrupted by disasters.

The holidays just finished so people were back at work and kids returned to schools. Polish diplomats were getting ready for the arrival of their Foreign Minister, Władysław Bartoszewski, whose visit was scheduled to begin the following day. They were also busy preparing for parliamentary

Ambassador Janusz Reiter
congratulates Senator Chuck Hagel
on receiving the
Commander Cross of the Order
of Merit of the Republic of Poland in 2007.
Photo by Richard Poremski.

Ambassador Robert Kupiecki
presenting the Commander
Cross of the Order of Merit of the
Republic of Poland to Mr. Allen
Paul, author of the book *Katyn:
The Untold Story of Stalin's
Polish Massacre*, April 29, 2009.
Photo by Mariusz Brymora.

Senator John McCain presented with the newly inaugurated crystal
White Eagle Award by Ambassador Ryszard Schnepf on May 20, 2015.
Photo by Richard Poremski.

elections due in 12 days. It seemed to be an ordinary Tuesday morning, September 11, 2001, when suddenly the evil struck. In the most tragic terrorist attack ever carried against America almost three thousand people were killed and over six thousand were injured. The country was paralyzed. All airports were shut down. Most federal offices as well as exchange, banks and universities were closed. Polish missions were in full attention and operation from the moment the planes struck their first goals. Following the attack, consuls were on duty 24/7 until the situation went back to normal. Special telephone lines were open so that the Polish citizens could report the missing relatives and seek information about casualties. Luckily, it turned out there were only six Polish Nationals who lost their lives in WTC towers. All officials of the Polish missions who were serving at that time in the United States agree that it was the day they will remember forever as it seemed war knocked on the doors of America.

The year 2010 marked the 70th anniversary of the Katyn Massacre (see footnote on p. 67). In the early hours of the morning on April 10, the Polish official delegation on board of a Tupolev TU-154 aircraft of the Polish Air Force was *en route* from Warsaw to attend an event commemorating the

Six weeks after the attack, the firefighters were still watering the ruins of the part of the Pentagon where one of the planes struck. Photo by Mariusz Brymora.

massacre. While attempting to land at Smolensk Airport in thick fog, with visibility reduced to about 1500 feet, the aircraft missed the runway, hit treetops and crashed into the ground killing all 96 passengers. Among them was the President of Poland Lech Kaczyński and his wife Maria, the last Polish President in Exile Ryszard Kaczorowski and many other senior political and military leaders. The Polish Foreign Service lost in the crash the deputy Minister of Foreign Affairs – Andrzej Kremer, the Chief of Diplomatic Protocol of the Polish MFA Mariusz Kazana and the Undersecretary of State at the Chancellery of the President and the former member of the Polish Embassy in Washington staff Mariusz Handzlik. The crash was the worst Polish national disaster since WWII.

* * *

Until recently, the youngest Polish diplomatic mission in the USA was the Consulate General in Los Angeles. For many years Chicago used to have jurisdiction over 28 states spread over the territory which was so huge that it was virtually impossible to cover. The number of people of Polish descent in California itself, estimated at nearly half a million, strengthened the expectations for a Polish mission there. Previously, the Americans were not too willing to grant permission for the Polish communist government to open one and would answer that the Soviet Consulate in San Francisco was a sufficient representation of the Soviet bloc. However, when Solidarity won the elections in Poland and the government of Tadeusz Mazowiecki was formed, the situation changed dramatically and Krzysztof Skubiszewski, the then Foreign Minister, was able to receive the American consent speedily. The agreement assumed that a Polish Consulate would be set up in Los Angeles and the Americans could open one in Gdańsk (in fact they never made use of this right). Tadeusz Wojnowski was sent to LA by the Ministry in Warsaw with the task to get things organized there. The offices that he rented to house the Consulate were located on the corner of Wilshire Boulevard and Normandie Avenue, right in the middle of the part of the city known as Koreatown. Shortly afterwards, this location was to turn out to be very important for the future of the Consulate. After a few months of preparations on May 21, 1991, the Consulate was officially opened. About 300 guests, invited by the first Consul General Jan Szewc, arrived for the ceremony. The guests of honor included the Polish Ambassador from

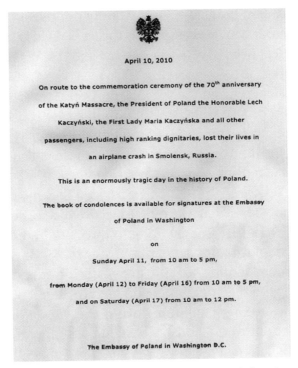

April 10, 2010

On route to the commemoration ceremony of the 70th anniversary of the Katyń Massacre, the President of Poland the Honorable Lech Kaczyński, the First Lady Maria Kaczyńska and all other passengers, including high ranking dignitaries, lost their lives in an airplane crash in Smolensk, Russia.

This is an enormously tragic day in the history of Poland.

The book of condolences is available for signatures at the Embassy of Poland in Washington

on

Sunday April 11, from 10 am to 5 pm,

from Monday (April 12) to Friday (April 16) from 10 am to 5 pm,

and on Saturday (April 17) from 10 am to 12 pm.

The Embassy of Poland in Washington D.C.

The announcement of the Polish Embassy informing about the tragedy at Smolensk on April 10, 2010. Photo by Richard Poremski.

The fence of the Embassy premises in the days immediately following the plane crash at Smolensk. Photo by Richard Poremski.

Washington and Tom Bradley – the Mayor of Los Angeles. It was a Polish day in LA for more than one reason. On this very day LOT Polish Airlines opened a direct connection between Warsaw and Los Angeles and the first Polish plane landed on LAX airport just when the Polish Consulate was being opened. The holiday was quickly over and the Consulate started to perform the normal tasks of a consular mission. In this case it had to start with a gigantic job of transferring from Chicago the personal records of all the Polish citizens who lived on the territory under the jurisdiction of the newly established consular district, i.e. 15 western states.

A year later, on April 29, 1992, this part of LA became the scene of the Rodney King riots after a jury acquitted four police officers accused of beating a black motorist Rodney King following a high-speed pursuit. Thousands of people in Koreatown rioted over the six days following the verdict. Widespread looting, assault, arson, and murder occurred, while property damage totaled one billion dollars. In all, 63 people died and over two thousand were injured during the riots. Moreover, it all happened next door to the Polish Consulate. The Department of State ordered the evacuation of the Consulate and the staff could not return to the office for the duration of the riots. This situation started immediate consideration of changing the location, which ended in 1995 with a move to the current offices at 12400 Wilshire Boulevard. The Consulate has been happily operating there until today and after a major redecoration project carried out in 2014 it is probably one of the most modern offices Polish diplomats work at.

The time after the Solidarity's victory in 1989 meant a new beginning for Poland in every aspect of life, including public diplomacy. The primary aim of public diplomacy is to foster understanding and support for the national interest and policies of the Polish Government among ordinary people of the receiving state or, in other words, to "to win the hearts and change the minds" of foreign societies. A crucial role in disseminating comprehensive knowledge of Poland, Polish history and national heritage, as well as promoting Poland's contemporary contribution to the world culture is carried out by the network of Polish Institutes – special missions operating in the field of public diplomacy. Right at the turn of the 20th century, in mid-2000, the Polish Cultural Institute started operating in the Empire State Building in New York City as a special form of the diplomatic presence of Poland in the U.S.

When visiting the State of Oregon in summer 2016 the then Minister of Foreign Affairs Witold Waszczykowski asked the Consul General in LA in which cities of the United States Poland should open new consulates. In reply, he was given two suggestions: Houston, TX and Seattle, WA. A year and a half later, the Consulate General in Houston was opened as the fourth Polish consular mission in America and the first expansion of Polish consular network in almost 25 years. Similarly to many other consulates in the city, it is located at a rental space in a multi story building in a prestigious district of Uptown, Houston. With jurisdiction over seven states it serves a few hundred thousand people of Polish descent. However, a special focus of this Consulate is to be on economic diplomacy and fostering cooperation in the field of energy supply.

The current Polish Ambassador to the United States, Piotr Wilczek, was nominated to this post right after the Presidential elections in November 2016. In fact, he submitted a copy of his credentials at the Department of State just two days after America had decided to elect Donald Trump as its 45th President. Of course, the White House was still occupied by the Obamas but it turned out that the outgoing President had not received any new ambassadors since September. A few weeks passed and the Department of State realized that there was a group of 15 ambassadors in town who did not have a chance to present their credentials and that if it remained like that, they would not be able to attend the upcoming Presidential Inauguration. The solution was… an Executive Order issued by President Obama accepting the representatives of all 15 countries. This way Ambassador Wilczek and his colleagues from India, Iraq, Jamaica or Montenegro (just to name a few) constitute a unique group in the history of diplomacy of those who were accredited by correspondence. Only after the President's Inauguration, the Polish Ambassador and all other members of his group were received by President Trump at the Blair House for a welcome lunch.

A short comparison of the main goals of the diplomatic missions of the first Polish Envoy in 1919 and the current host of the Embassy shows how completely different the situation of Poland was at that time from what it is today.

When Prince Lubomirski came to America, Poland was just starting her new life. Devastated by the partitions, economically underdeveloped and ethnically mixed, the country was in desperate need of stabilization and development. In

Pursuant to the Authority vested in me by the Constitution of the United States, I accept the Letter of Credence for Piotr Antoni Wilczek as Ambassador of the Republic of Poland to the United States of America and accept him as Ambassador Extraordinary and Plenipotentiary of the Republic of Poland, and acknowledge receipt of the Letter of Recall of his predecessor. I welcome Ambassador Wilczek as a member of the diplomatic corps in Washington and express our Government's desire to advance our common agenda and to deepen the strong and abiding friendship between our countries.

THE WHITE HOUSE,

January 18, 2017.

Scan of the Executive Order of President Barack Obama
accepting the credentials of Ambassador Piotr Wilczek.

a statement he gave at the Gotham Hotel on the day he arrived in New York, the Envoy described the country's situation and hopes saying:

"Poland now has to recover from its slavery of over 100 years, and has to achieve in a short time social betterment and material improvement which other nations have accomplished progressively in many years. American skill and energy can help us accomplish this task, and I am sure they will not be denied to us. (…) Today we are asking this great American nation to give us a share of the love which she received from our countrymen."

When, after more than half a year since taking up his duties, Prince Lubomirski finally presented his credentials at the White House, he said to President Wilson:

"It is my great hope that my presence here may do something further to strengthen the ties of friendship and trust that already bind the hearts of the people of Poland and the people of the United States, and that in some measure I may be one agency through which an even greater and fuller cooperation may be had between the Government of the Republic of Poland and the Government of the United States."

Ambassador Wilczek went to Washington almost one hundred years later to represent there a strong Central European Parliamentary Democracy, a leading member of the EU whose economy is the 6th strongest in the Union, and a loyal member of NATO Alliance which actively takes part in all most important peace missions of the Pact and contributes deployment of troops to the democratic coalitions fighting the world terrorism.

In June 2016, at a conference in Wrocław when presenting his proposal for the future of Polish-U.S. relations, prof. Wilczek made the following his priorities:

"We need to maintain the best aspects of Polish diplomatic activity in the US: the US contributing to Poland's democratic transition; the training of the new Polish military elite in the U.S. and help in the structural transformation of the Polish army; the development of economic relations; building on the experience of prominent Poles residing in the US; strengthening relations with members of American political elite who are friendly towards Poland; cooperation with top American think-tanks and the presence of Polish content on the K-Street Corridor."

Consequently, when presenting the main objectives of his mission before the Foreign Affairs Commission of the Polish Sejm, Ambassador Wilczek was talking about maintaining the existing dynamics of the mutual cooperation and prompt implementation of already taken decisions. As an example, he indicated the decision of the Warsaw NATO Summit from July 2016 to strengthen the eastern flank of the Pact by deploying more American troops in Poland. He also mentioned increasing economic cooperation between the two countries, which still have not reached a satisfactory level despite our trade exchange exceeding the value of 10 billion dollars. Developing cooperation in science and innovation were also among Ambassador Wilczek's priorities. Intensification of Polish efforts in the field of public diplomacy and cooperation with the Polish diaspora in America topped up the list of objectives that the current crew of the Polish Embassy is working on.

U.S. Assistant Secretary of State Wess Mitchell and Ambassador
Piotr Wilczek during the presentation of the national anthems
at the Polish residence on May 10, 2018. Photo by Richard Poremski.

To complete the present panorama of Polish diplomatic activity in America it is worth noting that on January 1, 2018, Poland began its two-year term as a non-permanent member of the UN Security Council for the sixth time. Considering the world's situation, it described the main objectives for the current term as strengthening the position of the international law, protecting human rights in miltary conflicts and supporting peaceful settlements of disputes.

* * *

After the transformations of 1989 Poland became one of the closest allies of the United States and every Polish Government enjoyed very good relations with the respective Administration at the White House. Contacts between the two states became very intense which is reflected in numerous visits of their leaders in Warsaw and Washington. The Embassy and all Polish Consulates General co-operate with the American Government on everyday basis. Poland is a stalwart European ally and one of the United States' strongest partners in fostering transatlantic security and promoting democracy and freedom in Europe and around the world. Poland also is the United States' largest commercial partner in Central Europe.

"The close cooperation between our two countries was stressed in the 'Declaration on Polish-American Strategic Partnership' signed at the White House by Presidents Trump and Duda on Sept. 18, 2018. The language of the Declaration underscores that our bilateral relationship is built on a foundation of respect for and commitment to, common democratic values and principles, including freedom, independent institutions and human rights. It also emphasizes the strong ties and common interests between our countries in the areas of security and defense, energy, trade and investment, research and innovation. As ambassadors for our respective countries, we will work tirelessly to ensure that the objectives of the Declaration are carried out through concrete actions.

Today, a century after Poland regained its independence, 30 years after the fall of communism and 20 years after Poland joined NATO, the bond between the United States and Poland is stronger than ever, and we are ready to face the next 100 years together."[66]

The Consulate General of Poland in New York in 2002 – view from Empire State Building Observatory. Photo by Mariusz Brymora.

66 Excerpts from the joint statement of Ambassadors Georgette Mosbacher and Piotr Wilczek from November 10, 2018 on the occasion of the 100th anniversary of Poland's regaining independence.

Embassy building with a banner celebrating 30th anniversary
of the birth of Solidarity – summer 2010. Photo by Richard Poremski.

The building with the offices of the Consulate General
of Poland in Los Angeles (2014). Photo by Małgorzata Cup.

The building with the offices of the Polish Consulate
General in Houston (2018). Photo by Piotr Rogulski.

Afterword

When the American state was being born in the years between ratifying the Declaration of Independence (1776) and signing the Constitution (1787), the Americans were greatly helped in their fight for independence by Kosciuszko and Pulaski, who earned themselves the title of "heroes of the two nations." Poland followed the American example becoming the second country in the world to adopt a modern Constitution.[67] It may seem that it was the ideal time to start and develop close relations between the two countries. Unfortunately, shortly afterwards, the partition of Poland (1795) wiped the country off the map of Europe for well over a century. Thereby the dream of building a strong Poland and its ties with America disappeared. Only after Poland had regained independence at the conclusion of World War I, the United States recognized the new state and the diplomatic relations between the two nations were started without further ado.

For most of the time, these relations remained very good. The most unfortunate moment came at the end of World War II when America accepted the Yalta Agreement and thus the new order in Europe, which left Poland on the wrong side of the division curtain. The years of Polish People's Republic (when Poland was a satellite country of Moscow) was

---

67 Polish Constitution of May 3, 1791 established constitutional monarchy, abolished elections of kings, introducing hereditary throne, established government called the Guardian of Laws and introduced responsibility of the ministers to the Sejm (Polish Parliament). Catholicism was considered the reigning religion. However, other denominations were assured tolerance. The privileged position of the gentry was maintained while considerable rights were granted to burghers. Peasants were recognized as a part of the nation for the first time in Polish history and they were assured protection of law. Unfortunately, the Polish State at that time proved too weak to hold such ambitious provisions for a long time. The Constitution was in effect for only two years before Poland lost its independence as a result of partitions.

also a difficult time of coldness in the mutual relationship, which was characterized by kind of a double American policy – a more official and restrictive toward the Polish authorities, and a more friendly and open toward the people. The birth of Solidarity in Gdansk and the events which followed not only put Poland back on the path of democracy but also triggered a domino effect and eventually led to the fall of the Berlin Wall and the return of Central and East European countries to the democratic family. This process was greatly helped by the United States which offered all kinds of aid to suppress communism. Regaining sovereignty by Poland restored its ties with the U.S. in their best form and transformed the mutual relations into the level of a close political and military alliance. The Polish authorities designated the United States their strategic partner and the relations with America became one of the priorities of Poland's foreign policy.

The current diplomatic representation of Poland in the U.S. is headed by the Embassy in Washington D.C., which supervises the activity of its Consular Division as well as four Consulates General based in Chicago, New York, Los Angeles and Houston. In fulfilling their tasks, the Polish career missions are greatly helped by a network of c. 20 Honorary Consulates stretched from Alaska to the Bahamas, from Hawaii to Massachusetts, and from Florida to the State of Washington.

Throughout the one hundred years of mutual diplomatic ties, Poland has posted 20 ambassadors to the United States (including envoys, but not counting *charge d'affaires*; two of them – Ciechanowski and Spasowski – were in office twice). Over the years, the Polish missions acquired a good reputation in social circles of respective American cities for not only representing the country's political interests but also fulfilling the role of keeping in touch with Polish Americans. Politics and business is not all that is involved in diplomatic life and activity. Diplomats also find themselves working hard to keep Polish culture alive in America – the land of immigrants, where people of Polish descent constitute about 3% of the nation's population.

Looking ahead, the new chapter of Polish diplomatic presence in the United States of America is promising to be as interesting as the one whose end is marked by the centennial of establishing the relations. Despite all the challenges that the contemporary world has to face, it is everybody's "cherished hope," as the first Polish Envoy to the United States put it almost exactly one hundred years ago, "that the relations between two great Republics will forever remain on the same high plane established by their hereditary traditions."[68]

---

68 Remarks of Prince Kazimierz Lubomirski at the presentation of his credentials to the President of the United States. Source: Polish Embassy in Washington Archives, the Hoover Institution, Stanford University.

Appendix

MINISTERS OF FOREIGN AFFAIRS OF POLAND

MINISTERS OF THE SECOND REPUBLIC

Tytus Filipowicz	November 16, 1918–November 17, 1918
Leon Wasilewski	November 17, 1918–January 16, 1919
Ignacy Jan Paderewski	January 16, 1919–December 9, 1919
Władysław Wróblewski	December 13, 1919–December 16, 1919
Stanisław Patek	December 16, 1919–December 9, 1920
Eustachy Sapieha	June 23, 1920–May 24, 1921
Jan Dąbski	May 24, 1921–June 11, 1921
Konstanty Skirmunt	June 11, 1921–June 6, 1922
Gabriel Narutowicz	June 28, 1922–December 14, 1922
Aleksander Skrzyński	December 16, 1922–May 26, 1923
Marian Seyda	May 28, 1923–October 27, 1923
Roman Dmowski	October 27, 1923–December 14, 1923
Karol Bertoni	December 19, 1923–January 19, 1924
Maurycy Zamoyski	January 19, 1924–July 27, 1924
Aleksander Skrzyński	July 27, 1924–May 5, 1926
Kajetan Dzierżykraj-Morawski	May 10, 1926–May 15, 1926
August Zaleski	May 15, 1926–June 25, 1926
August Zaleski	June 25, 1926–November 2, 1932
Józef Beck	November 2, 1932–September 30, 1939

MINISTERS OF THE GOVERNMENT IN EXILE

August Zaleski	September 30, 1939–July 25, 1941
Edward Bernard Raczyński	August 22, 1941–July 14, 1943
Tadeusz Romer	July 14, 1943–November 24, 1944

Adam Tarnowski	November 29, 1944–February 10, 1949
Mieczysław Sokołowski	April 7, 1949–December 8, 1953
Aleksander Zawisza	August 8, 1955–June 11, 1970
Jerzy Gawenda	July 20, 1970–July 14, 1972
Jan Starzewski	July 18, 1972–January 25, 1973
Jerzy Gawenda	January 1973–December 1973
Bronisław Hełczyński	January 29, 1974–August 5, 1976
Zygmunt Zawadowski	August 5, 1976–September 1, 1978
Kazimierz Sabbat	June 20, 1979–April 7, 1986
Zygmunt Szkopiak	1986–December 20, 1990

MINISTERS OF THE POLISH PEOPLE'S REPUBLIC

Edward Osóbka-Morawski	July 21, 1944–May 2, 1945
Wincenty Rzymowski	May 2, 1945–February 7, 1947
Zygmunt Modzelewski	February 8, 1947–March 20, 1951
Stanisław Skrzeszewski	March 20, 1951–April 27, 1956
Adam Rapacki	April 27, 1956–December 22, 1968
Stefan Jędrychowski	December 22, 1968–December 22, 1971
Stefan Olszowski	December 22, 1971–December 2, 1976
Emil Wojtaszek	December 2, 1976–August 24, 1980
Józef Czyrek	August 24, 1980–July 21, 1982
Stefan Olszowski	July 21, 1982–November 12, 1985
Marian Orzechowski	November 12, 1985–June 17, 1988
Tadeusz Olechowski	June 17, 1988–September 12, 1989

MINISTERS OF THE REPUBLIC OF POLAND

Krzysztof Skubiszewski	September 12, 1989–October 26, 1993
Andrzej Olechowski	October 26, 1993–March 6, 1995
Władysław Bartoszewski	March 7, 1995–December 22, 1995
Dariusz Rosati	December 29, 1995–October 31, 1997
Bronisław Geremek	October 31, 1997–June 30, 2000
Władysław Bartoszewski	June 30, 2000–October 19, 2001
Włodzimierz Cimoszewicz	October 19, 2001–January 5, 2005
Adam Rotfeld	January 5, 2005–October 31, 2005
Stefan Meller	October 31, 2005–May 9, 2006

Anna Fotyga	May 9, 2006–November 16, 2007
Radosław Sikorski	November 16, 2007–September 22, 2014
Grzegorz Schetyna	September 22, 2014–November 16, 2015
Witold Waszczykowski	November 16, 2015–January 9, 2018
Jacek Czaputowicz	from January 9, 2018

HEADS OF THE POLISH MISSIONS
IN THE UNITED STATES

THE EMBASSY IN WASHINGTON D.C.

Kazimierz Lubomirski 1919–1921
Michał Kwapiszewski (*chargé d'affaires*) 1922
Władysław Wróblewski 1922–1925
Jan Ciechanowski 1925–1929
Tytus Filipowicz 1929–1932
Władysław Sokołowski (*chargé d'affaires*) 1932–1933
Stanisław Patek 1933–1935
Władysław Sokołowski (*chargé d'affaires*) 1935–1936
Jerzy Potocki 1936–1940
Jan Ciechanowski 1940–1945
Janusz Żółtowski (*chargé d'affaires*) 1945
Oskar Lange 1945–1947
Józef Winiewicz 1947–1955
Romuald Spasowski 1955–1961
Edward Drożniak 1961–1967
Jerzy Michałowski 1967–1972
Witold Trąmpczyński 1972–1977
Romuald Spasowski 1978–1981
Zdzisław Ludwiczak (*chargé d'affaires*) 1982–1988
Jan Kinast 1988–1990
Kazimierz Dziewanowski 1990–1993
Maciej Kozłowski (*chargé d'affaires*) 1993–1994
Jerzy Koźmiński 1994–2000
Przemysław Grudziński 2000–2005
Janusz Reiter 2005–2007
Wojciech Flera (*chargé d'affaires*) 2007–2008

Robert Kupiecki 2008–2012
Ryszard Schnepf 2012–2016
Piotr Wilczek from 2016

THE POLISH MISSION AT THE UNITED NATIONS

Oskar Lange 1945–1947
Juliusz Kat-Suchy 1947–1951
Henryk Birecki 1951–1956
Jerzy Michałowski 1956–1960
Bohdan Lewandowski 1960–1966
Bohdan Tomorowicz 1966–1968
Eugeniusz Kułaga 1969–1975
Henryk Jaroszek 1975–1980
Ryszard Frelek 1980–1981
Eugeniusz Wyzner 1981–1982
Włodzimierz Natorf 1982–1985
Eugeniusz Noworyta 1985–1989
Stanisław Pawlak 1989–1991
Robert Mroziewicz 1991–1992
Zbigniew Włosowicz 1993–1997
Eugeniusz Wyzner 1998–1999
Janusz Stańczyk 2000–2004
Andrzej Towpik 2004–2010
Witold Sobków 2010–2012
Ryszard Sarkowicz 2012–2014
Bogusław Winid 2014–2017
Joanna Wronecka from 2017

THE CONSULATE GENERAL IN NEW YORK CITY

Konstanty Buszczyński 1919
Jerzy Barthel de Weydenthal 1919–1920
Zdzisław Kurnikowski 1920
Stefan Grotowski 1920–1925
Sylwester Gruszka 1925–1928
Tadeusz Marynowski 1928
Eugeniusz Rozwadowski 1928–1929

Mieczysław Marchlewski 1929–1935

Jerzy Matusiński 1935

Sylwester Gruszka 1935–1940

Sylwin Strakacz 1941–1945

Eugeniusz Rozwadowski 1945–1947

Jan Galewicz 1947–1953

Kazimierz Ciaś 1970–1974

Zbigniew Dembowski 1975–1978

Maksymilian Służewski 1979

Kazimierz Ciaś 1979–1981

Waldemar Lipka-Chudzik 1981–1990

Jerzy Surdykowski 1990–1996

Dariusz Jadowski 1997–2001

Agnieszka Magdziak-Miszewska 2001–2005

Krzysztof Kasprzyk 2005–2010

Ewa Junczyk–Ziomecka 2010–2014

Urszula Gacek 2014–2016

Katarzyna Padło 2016–2017

Maciej Golubiewski from 2017

THE CONSULATE GENERAL IN CHICAGO

Zygmunt Nowicki 1920–1922

Jerzy Barthel de Weydenthal 1923–1926

Kazimierz Kurnikowski 1926–1929

Aleksander Szczepański 1929–1930

Tytus Zbyszewski 1931–1934

Wacław Gawroński 1934–1939

Karol Ripa 1940–1944

Juliusz Szygowski 1945

Stefan Rogoziński 1945–1947

Marian Cieplak 1947–1949

Zygmunt Fabisiak 1949–1952

Wojciech Albrycht 1952–1954

Włodzimierz Zawadzki 1959–1963

Adolf Kita 1963–1967

Bogumił Sujka 1968

Wojciech Jaskot 1969–1972
Romuald Czubacki 1972–1975
Wojciech Jaskot 1975–1979
Jerzy Janowski 1979
Juliusz Biały 1979–1984
Jan Rabś 1984–1988
Tadeusz Czerwiński 1988–1990
Hubert Romanowski 1990–1991
Andrzej Jaroszyński 1991–1992
Michał Grocholski 1992–1997
Ryszard Sarkowicz 1997–2001
Franciszek Adamczyk 2001–2005
Jarosław Łasiński 2005–2006
Paweł Pietrasieński 2006–2007
Zygmunt Matynia 2007–2012
Paulina Kapuścińska 2012–2016
Piotr Janicki from 2016

THE CONSULATE IN DETROIT

Jerzy Barthel de Weydenthal 1921–1923
Sylwester Gruszka 1923–1926
Władysław Kozłowski 1926–1930
Jan Byszewski 1931–1932
Stanisław Angerman 1942–1945
Olgierd Langer 1945–1947
Tadeusz Frymar 1947–1952
Zygmunt Krawczyk 1952–1953

THE CONSULATE IN PITTSBURGH

Kazimierz Kurnikowski 1920–1926
Artur Marian Ocetkiewicz 1924–1932
Jan Byszewski 1932–1933
Jerzy Matusiński 1933–1935
Karol Ripa 1935–1938
Heliodor Sztark 1938–1945
Roman Kwiecień 1945–1947
Zygmunt Fabisiak 1948–1949

THE CONSULATE IN BUFFALO

Stanisław Manduk 1920–1926
Stanisław Rosicki 1926–1929
Tadeusz Marynowski 1930–1932

THE CONSULATE IN SAN FRANCISCO

Karol Pindór 1920–1921
Władysław Sokołowski 1943–1945

THE CONSULATE GENERAL IN LOS ANGELES

Jan Szewc 1991–1995
Maciej Krych 1995–1999
Krzysztof Kasprzyk 1999–2003
Krystyna Tokarska-Biernacik 2003–2007
Paulina Kapuścińska 2007–2009
Joanna Kozińska-Frybes 2009–2013
Mariusz Brymora 2013–2017
Jarosław Łasiński from 2018

THE CONSULATE GENERAL IN HOUSTON

Robert Rusiecki from 2018

The Kosciuszko Foundation

Founded in 1925, the Kosciuszko Foundation is dedicated to promote educational and cultural exchanges between the United States and Poland and to increase American understanding of Polish culture and history. It is a national not-for-profit, nonpartisan, and nonsectarian organization. The Kosciuszko Foundation is a membership organization, which is supported by contributions from foundations, corporations, and individuals who share the Foundation's mission.

The founder of the Foundation and the author of the original idea of granting scholarships to young Poles was Stephen Mizwa, a Polish immigrant, who on the basis of his own experience knew how important financial support was for the young who wanted to acquire good education. With the 150th anniversary of Kosciuszko's arrival in America approaching, Mizwa sought to create "a living memorial to Tadeusz Kosciuszko." In 1925, The Kosciuszko Foundation was incorporated in New York to raise funds and grant financial aid to deserving Polish students to study in America and American students desiring to study in Poland, to encourage and aid the

exchange of professors, scholars and lecturers between Poland and the United States, and to cultivate closer intellectual and cultural ties between the two countries.

In 1928, the Kosciuszko Foundation hosted a dinner at New York's Commodore Hotel to honor Paderewski, and by 1933, the Foundation began holding an annual fundraising ball to support its operations. Staring in the early part of 1945, Mizwa started his search for a permanent headquarters for the Foundation. After six months of bargaining, his deal to buy the 1917 Van Alen mansion from Mrs. Rufus Peterson, was the greatest achievement in the Foundation's history because it gave *Polonia* a headquarters in the most affluent and desirable neighborhood in New York.

Today the Foundation's work reaches audiences throughout the United States, through its headquarters in New York City and its regional Chapters in Chicago, Denver, Houston, Philadelphia, Pittsburgh, Springfield, Buffalo, Ohio as well as through its National Advisory Council. It awards up to $1 million annually in fellowships and grants to graduate students, scholars, scientists, professionals, and artists, and promotes Polish culture in America.

In 2010, Fundacja Kościuszkowska Polska was founded whose goal is to foster and promote in Poland the intellectual, cultural and educational exchange between the two countries.

The latest addition to the Foundation is its Diplomatic Advisory Council consisting of former Polish and American diplomats who have served both the countries. The Council was inaugurated in April 2019 and shall serve in an advisory capacity to the Board of Trustees.

Photos by Anna Fedisz

About the Author

MARIUSZ M. BRYMORA – Polish diplomat. Prior to joining the Foreign Service, he worked as an academic teacher and translator of English. His literary translations include short stories by Bernard Malamud published by Wydawnictwo Literackie in Kraków in 1989. From 1994 until 1998, he served as a Councilman and then the Deputy Mayor in his native city of Radom, Poland.

He has been a member of the Foreign Service since 1999 and served as Deputy Consul General in Chicago (1999–2003), Public Affairs Councilor of the Embassy of Poland in Washington D.C. (2005–2009), and Consul General in Los Angeles (2013–2017). While in Warsaw, he was the Deputy Director of the Department of Public and Cultural Diplomacy of Ministry of Foreign Affairs where he supervised the promotional activity of Polish diplomatic missions.

He is the co-author and editor of *400 Years of Polish Immigrants in America* – the album published in 2008 to celebrate the 400th anniversary of the first Poles' arrival at Jamestown, Virginia. He wrote a short history of *The Embassy of Poland in Washington D.C.*, published in 2009. He also supervised the screenplay and production of *Polska? Tak!* – a short documentary on Poland's image as seen through the eyes of the world's greatest cultural celebrities.

"Quite often in America you realize that you must say things that are most obvious to you but completely unknown to your listener. *One Hundred Years of Polish Diplomatic Presence in the United States: 1919–2019* is meant to celebrate the centennial of Polish American diplomatic ties but also to share with the people in America some of the things that we Poles know only too well."

Text: Mariusz M. Brymora
Proofreading: Roman S. Czarny and Filip Brymora
Graphic design: Janusz Barecki
Preprint: Studio Kolor, Rudna Mała
Printed by READ ME, Łódź

Image on the front cover by Arthur Szyk (1894–1951),
a Polish-Jewish artist.
Reproduced with the cooperation of the Szyk Family
and Irvin Ungar.

In anticipation of the 1939 World's Fair in New York, the government of
Poland commissioned Arthur Szyk to paint the large series *The Glorious
Days of the Polish-American Fraternity*, which examined the relationship
between Poland and the United States through significant contributions
made by individual Poles to the history of the U.S. The work on the front
cover, one of twenty in the collection, celebrates the friendship between
President Woodrow Wilson and Ignacy Paderewski, who both worked
for freedom and democracy. The original art hung in the Polish Pavilion
at the World's Fair and was reproduced on postcards printed in Kraków,
which were shipped in vast quantities to New York on the last pre-WWII
voyage of the Polish liner *Batory* to be distributed at the Polish pavilion
of the World's Fair.

Printed in Poland

ISBN 978-83-7576-425-3

Publisher
BOSZ Szymanik i wspólnicy sp. jawna
38-722 Olszanica 311, Poland
Office: 14 Przemysłowa Street, 38-600 Lesko, Poland
Phone: +48 13 469 90 00
office@bosz.com.pl
www.bosz.com.pl

BOSZ

Special thanks
to the Kosciuszko Foundation
in New York for supporting
this edition.